Adobe Type 1 Font Format

Adobe Systems Incorporated

D0921958

Addison-Wesley Publishing Company, Inc.
Reading, Massachusetts • Menlo Park, California • New York
Don Mills, Ontario • Wokingham, England • Amsterdam
Bonn • Sydney • Singapore • Tokyo • Madrid • San Juan

Library of Congress Cataloging-in-Publication Data

Adobe type 1 font format / Adobe Systems Incorporated.
    p. cm
   Includes index
   ISBN 0-201-57044-0
   1. PostScript (Computer program language)   2. Adobe
Type 1 font (Computer program) I. Adobe Systems.
QA76.73.P67A36 1990
686.2'2544536—dc20   90-42516

Printed in the United States of America.
Published simultaneously in Canada.

The information in this book is furnished for informational use only, is subject to change without notice, and should not be construed as a commitment by Adobe Systems Incorporated. Adobe Systems Incorporated assumes no responsibility or liability for any errors or inaccuracies that may appear in this book. The software described in this book is furnished under license and may only be used or copied in accordance with the terms of such license.

Please remember that existing font software programs that you may desire to access as a result of information described in this book may be protected under copyright law. The unauthorized use or modification of any existing font software program could be a violation of the rights of the author. Please be sure you obtain any permission required from such authors.

PostScript, the PostScript logo, Display PostScript, Adobe, and the Adobe logo are trademarks of Adobe Systems Incorporated registered in the U.S. Adobe Type Manager is a trademark of Adobe Systems Incorporated. IBM is a registered trademark of International Business Machines Corporation. Macintosh and LaserWriter are registered trademarks of Apple Computer, Inc. Helvetica and Optima are trademarks of Linotype AG and/or its subsidiaries. ITC Stone is a registered trademark of International Typeface Corporation. Other brand or product names are the trademarks or registered trademarks of their respective holders.

ABCDEFGHIJ-MW-943210
First printing, August 1990, Version 1.1

Contents

CHAPTER 1

Introduction

This document describes the organization of the Adobe Type 1 font format and how to create a Type 1 font program. A Type 1 font program is actually a special case of a PostScript® language program. The PostScript interpreter renders the font intelligently, in a device-independent manner. This allows a font developer to create one font program that can be rendered on a wide variety of devices and at many different resolutions.

- A Type 1 font program consists of a clear text (ASCII) portion, and an encoded and encrypted portion.

- The PostScript language commands used in a Type 1 font program must conform to a much stricter syntax than do "normal" PostScript language programs.

- Type 1 font programs can include special "hints" that make their representation as exact as possible on a wide variety of devices and pixel densities.

This document explains the required contents of the clear and encrypted portions of a Type 1 font program, reveals the font encryption and decryption algorithms, provides syntax information, and explains how to declare hints when creating Type 1 font programs.

- Chapter 1 discusses some background issues about Type 1 font programs and their differences from Type 3 font programs.

- Chapter 2 explains the different parts of the PostScript language program that makes up a font program.

- Chapter 3 describes general terminology and how the different features that make up the characters in a font program are constructed.

- Chapter 4 provides several tips on managing the technical part of design aesthetics.

- Chapter 5 explains the contents of the **Private** dictionary.

- Chapter 6 explains the contents of the **CharStrings** dictionary, explains charstring number and command encoding, and lists the commands used in Type 1 charstrings and their encodings.

- Chapter 7 discloses the method of encrypting and decrypting Type 1 font programs.

- Chapter 8 shows how subroutines can be used for font program space requirement reduction and hint substitution.

- Chapter 9 describes the special organization of synthetic and hybrid font programs.

- Chapter 10 provides necessary information to ensure compatibility with Adobe Type Manager™ (ATM™) software.

- The appendices contain lists of dictionary entries, commands, and PostScript language code that you may wish to include in your own font programs.

1.1 What Is a Type 1 Font Program?

The PostScript language has changed the way computers display and print documents. This language unifies text and graphics by treating letter shapes as general graphic objects. Since letters are used so frequently in printed images, the PostScript language has special operators to handle collections of letter shapes conveniently. These collections are called *fonts*; each font usually consists of letters and symbols whose shapes share certain stylistic properties.

The complete specification for the PostScript language, including information on how font programs are organized, appears in the *PostScript Language Reference Manual*, published by Addison-Wesley. In addition to the font format that is described in the *PostScript Language Reference Manual* (commonly known as "Type 3 font format" or "user-defined font format"), the PostScript interpreter also accepts a font format, called the *Type 1 font format*, that is not part of the PostScript language definition and is not fully described in the *PostScript Language Reference Manual*.

Type 1 font programs have several advantages over Type 3 font programs.

- Type 1 font programs are more compact.

- The PostScript interpreter uses special rasterization algorithms for Type 1 font programs that result in better looking output—especially at small sizes and low resolutions.

- Type 1 font programs contain *hints* that indicate special features of character shapes not directly expressible by the basic PostScript language operators.

The special rasterization algorithm and the hints for the Type 1 font format that the rasterization algorithm uses are directed at features common to collections of letter shapes. The special rasterization algorithm and the hints aim to preserve baselines, letter heights, stem weights, and other such features. Thus, the Type 1 format is excellent for characters intended to be read as text. Company logotypes and other symbols are candidates for the Type 1 font format only insofar as they are letter-like. While a graphic symbol may benefit from being made into a character in a font, extremely complicated graphic constructions are better served by the Type 3 font format as described in the *PostScript Language Reference Manual*.

1.2 What This Document Does

The Type 1 font format is a subset (and extension) of the PostScript language, with its own syntactical rules. This document explains how to create a Type 1 font program that will run properly in the PostScript interpreter and with other Type 1 font rendering software such as Adobe Type Manager. It also gives a developer the information necessary to decrypt and understand the organization of existing Type 1 font programs (such as the font software included in the Adobe® Type Library). This document assumes familiarity with the *PostScript Language Reference Manual*, especially the information about font programs.

Note *Although Type 1 font format elements are fully explained here, this document does not include any algorithms that achieve the results specified; for example, it does not include details of the rendering algorithm used by Adobe's PostScript interpreter.*

Some personal computer file systems require special formats for disk files that differ from the ASCII text format described here. The Apple Macintosh® and the IBM® PC are two such systems. This document does not discuss the details of formats used by such file systems; these formats can be derived from the ASCII font program information described here. Special file formats for these and other file systems are discussed in Technical Note #5040, *Supporting Downloadable PostScript Fonts*, available from the Adobe Systems developer support group.

1.3 Versions and Compatibility

The PostScript interpreter has undergone continual enhancement since its debut in late 1984. During this time, Adobe Systems has changed both the PostScript interpreter implementation and the features of the Type 1 font format. These changes are generally compatible with all versions of the PostScript interpreter.

There are several notes in this document about how specific font program features are treated in older versions of the PostScript interpreter. In some cases, information that was required by older versions of the PostScript interpreter for optimal rendering is no longer needed because more sophisticated algorithms are available in newer versions of the interpreter. In general, the rendering of typefaces described in the Type 1 font format will continue to look better with succeeding versions of the PostScript interpreter (without changing existing Type 1 font software at all) as Adobe Systems continues improving the PostScript interpreter.

Any future extensions of the Adobe Type 1 font format will be designed so that they may be ignored by the current generation of interpreters. These new features will often take the form of new dictionary entries; other extensions may involve subroutine calls that can be skipped safely. As long as interpreters for Type 1 font software are written to ignore such possible future features, these features will not cause trouble. Future extensions will be thoroughly described in revised versions of this document.

Some Type 1 font rendering software (such as the Adobe Type Manager product) take advantage of a particular stylized use of the PostScript language. As a result, a Type 1 font program must also adhere to these PostScript language usage conventions. The language resulting from these conventions is considerably more restricted than the PostScript language; a Type 1 font program can be read and executed by a PostScript interpreter, but not all PostScript language usage is acceptable in a Type 1 font program. These restrictions will be noted wherever necessary in this document, particularly in Chapter 10, "Adobe Type Manager Compatibility."

1.4 Copyrights for Type 1 Font Programs

Since Type 1 fonts are expressed as computer programs, they are copyrightable as is any other computer software. For some time, the copyright status of some types of typeface software was unclear, since typeface *designs* are not copyrightable in the United States. Because Type 1 fonts are computer programs rather than mere data depicting a typeface, they are clearly copyrightable.

A copyright on a Type 1 font program confers the same protection against unauthorized copying that other copyrightable works, including computer software, enjoy. The ideas expressed by copyrighted works are not protected; only the particular expression is. In the case of Type 1 font programs, the typeface shapes are not protected, but the program text is. A copyright on a Type 1 font program that generates a particular typeface does not preclude anyone from independently creating a different program for that same typeface.

The activity prevented by copyright is copying. Copying includes obvious acts such as verbatim copying and distribution. It also covers less obvious activities such as modification and translation into different forms. If the copyrighted work, in this case a Type 1 font program, is the source of these activities, then the activities are illegal if not authorized by the copyright holder.

Adobe Systems' Type 1 font programs are licensed for use on one or more devices (depending on the terms of particular licenses). These licenses would permit the use of a licensed program in a system that translates a Type 1 font program to some other format in the process of rendering, as long as a copy of the program (even in translated form) is not produced.

The personal computer software industry has benefitted greatly from copyright protection. Competition is keen, and users benefit from the efforts software developers have found to be worthwhile. Copyright protection gives the developer of a Type 1 font program the incentive to create excellent typeface programs. In turn, the user of Type 1 font programs can expect to have available the finest typeface software to choose from.

CHAPTER **2**

Font Program Organization

A font program written in the PostScript language is a program that is an organized collection of procedures describing character shapes. Elements of this collection are accessed by character code with the **show** operator, as described in the *PostScript Language Reference Manual*. Different font programs contain different amounts of diverse information, this information is collected into a dictionary. The dictionary contains required and optional entries, and is the data object that the PostScript interpreter references for all font operations.

2.1 Building Characters

Every *Type 3* (user-defined) font program requires a font dictionary entry named **BuildChar**, as described in the *PostScript Language Reference Manual*. The value associated with this name is a procedure that the PostScript interpreter calls whenever it needs to have a character built. The Type 3 **BuildChar** procedure is free to use whatever method it chooses to supply the PostScript interpreter with graphics commands to paint the character associated with a character code. Generally, **BuildChar** procedures operate by selecting a particular procedure for building a character from an array or from a dictionary of such procedures stored in the font dictionary.

In contrast, Type 1 font programs *implicitly* reference a special **BuildChar** procedure called *Type 1 BuildChar* that is internal to the PostScript interpreter. Consequently, there is no explicit entry named **BuildChar** in a Type 1 font dictionary; the fact that it is a Type 1 font program *implies* that it uses Type 1 BuildChar. In essence, the description of the Type 1 font format is the explanation of the functions of Type 1 BuildChar.

Type 1 BuildChar begins by using the character code as an index into the **Encoding** array in the font dictionary to obtain the name of the character to be built. This step is explained in the *PostScript Language Reference Manual*; among other advantages, it enables a user to re-encode a Type 1 font program by changing the **Encoding** array without changing anything else. Type 1 Build-Char then uses the name of the character to be built as a key in the **CharStrings** dictionary (contained in the font dictionary) to obtain a binary string. The string is an encoded and encrypted representation of a PostScript language program for that character's outline. Finally, Type 1 BuildChar calls a special version of **stroke** or **fill**, depending on the value of **PaintType** in the font dictionary, to create the character.

Note   *Because Type 1 font programs were originally produced and were carefully checked only within Adobe Systems, Type 1 BuildChar was designed with the expectation that only error-free Type 1 font programs would be presented to it. Consequently, Type 1 BuildChar does not protect itself against data inconsistencies and other problems. For example, Type 1 BuildChar does not issue error messages. As long as you follow the rules and suggestions given in this manual, your font programs will work. Deviations from the suggestions in this document are somewhat risky. Many problems are likely to be caught with an* **invalidfont** *error; more subtle problems may result in incorrect behavior by Type 1 BuildChar. Of course, any Type 1 font program produced should be thoroughly tested at many sizes and rotations, on several devices, and with Adobe Type Manager software before release.*

2.2 Font Dictionary

Constructing a Type 1 font program means constructing a special type of font dictionary. As with any PostScript language data object, a PostScript language program constructs this dictionary. A list of the required entries in a Type 1 font program is given in the *PostScript Language Reference Manual*, and includes the **CharStrings** and **Private** dictionaries, which are required in every Type 1 font program.

Figure 2a is a conceptual overview of a Type 1 font program; figure 2b shows the dictionary structure that the font program creates when it executes. The items contained in the figures are explained in this document.

Figure 2a. *Organization of a Type 1 font program*

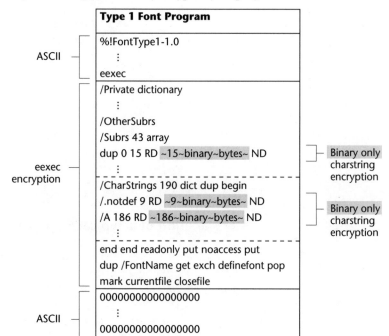

font dictionary	
/FontInfo	*dictionary*
/FontName	*name*
/Encoding	*array*
/PaintType	*integer*
/FontType	*integer*
/FontMatrix	*array*
/FontBBox	*array*
/UniqueID	*integer*
/Metrics	*dictionary*
/StrokeWidth	*number*
/Private	*dictionary*
/CharStrings	*dictionary*
(/FID)	*fontID*

/FontInfo dictionary	
/version	*string*
/Notice	*string*
/FullName	*string*
/FamilyName	*string*
/Weight	*string*
/ItalicAngle	*number*
/isFixedPitch	*boolean*
/UnderlinePosition	*number*
/UnderlineThickness	*number*

/CharStrings dictionary	
/A	*charstring*
/B	*charstring*
:	:
/.notdef	*charstring*

/Private dictionary	
/RD	*procedure*
/ND	*procedure*
/NP	*procedure*
/Subrs	*array*
/OtherSubrs	*array*
/UniqueID	*integer*
/BlueValues	*array*
/OtherBlues	*array*
/FamilyBlues	*array*
/FamilyOtherBlues	*array*
/BlueScale	*number*
/BlueShift	*integer*
/BlueFuzz	*integer*
/StdHW	*array*
/StdVW	*array*
/StemSnapH	*array*
/StemSnapV	*array*
/ForceBold	*boolean*
/LanguageGroup	*integer*
/password	*integer*
/lenIV	*integer*
/MinFeature	*array*
/RndStemUp	*boolean*

2.3   Explanation of a Typical Font Program

The program code that follows is a generalized example for a typical Adobe Type 1 font program. It is derived from the Symbol font program. Because many parts of a font definition are repetitive, much of the repetition in the following example has been omitted. The omitted portions are documented with comments. Items not explicitly discussed here are covered in the *PostScript Language Reference Manual*.

Example 1.

```
%!FontType1-1.0:  Symbol  001.003
%%CreationDate: Thu Apr 16 1987
%%VMusage: 27647 34029
% Copyright (c) 1985, 1987 Adobe Systems
% Incorporated. All rights reserved.
11 dict begin
/FontInfo 8 dict dup begin
/version (001.003) readonly def
/FullName (Symbol) readonly def
/FamilyName (Symbol) readonly def
/Weight (Medium) readonly def
/ItalicAngle 0 def
/isFixedPitch false def
/UnderlinePosition -98 def
/UnderlineThickness 54 def
end readonly def
/FontName /Symbol def
/PaintType 0 def
/FontType 1 def
/FontMatrix [0.001 0 0 0.001 0 0] readonly def
/Encoding 256 array
0 1 255 {1 index exch /.notdef put } for
dup 32 /space put
% . . .
% . . . repetitive assignments to Encoding array omitted
% . . .
dup 254 /bracerightbt put
readonly def
/FontBBox {-180 -293 1090 1010} readonly def
/UniqueID 6859 def
currentdict end
currentfile eexec
05f3acf73b42a65ec11a12df4c6e26
5306f37b5075f007986cdacc4cd13a
49703465ba20c83c12707f179c0586
3d27adc72767ec06a47e733401fa8d
% . . .
% . . . thousands of eexec-encrypted bytes omitted
% . . .
0000000000000000000000000000000
0000000000000000000000000000000
% . . .
% . . . many zeros omitted
% . . .
0000000000000000000000000000000
0000000000000000000000000000000
cleartomark
```

As seen in the preceding example, a Type 1 font program is a program written in the PostScript language. It begins with comments, some of which should be self-explanatory.

All Type 1 fonts must begin with the comment:

%!

This enables a file containing a PostScript program to be easily identified as such. It is important that every Type 1 font program—indeed, every PostScript language program—start with a "%!" comment; otherwise, it may not be given the appropriate handling in some operating system environments.

The remainder of the first line (after the "%!") should identify the file as a conforming Type 1 font program. A Type 1 font program conforms to the specified version of the Type 1 font format if the first line consists of the following characters:

%!FontType1-*SpecVersion*: *FontName* *FontVersion*

where the number *SpecVersion* is the version of the Adobe Type 1 font format to which the font program conforms (this document describes Version 1.1 of the *Adobe Type 1 Font Format*), *FontName* is the name of the font understood by the PostScript interpreter, and *FontVersion* is the version number of the font program. For example, the font program shown as an example in this document begins with:

%!FontType1-1.0: Symbol 001.003

Note *Application programs should also look for the form used by font programs from Adobe: "%!PS-AdobeFont-1.0: FontName version".*

The comment:

%%VMusage

is useful for application programs, not for the PostScript interpreter itself. The application program can use the information before downloading a font program to decide whether a given PostScript interpreter has enough VM storage remaining to accommodate this particular font program. A Type 1 font program manufacturer can determine the VM usage values by issuing a **vmstatus** command before and after downloading a font, and then again after downloading the same font a second time. The difference between the first and second numbers (before and after the first downloading) yields the second argument in the **%%VMusage** comment; the difference between the second and third (after the second download) give the first argument.

The larger number on this line indicates the amount of VM storage this font program will consume if it is the first to be downloaded; the smaller number indicates the minimum amount of VM this font program will need. The numbers are not equal because some items, such as names, can share VM storage in some versions of the PostScript interpreter. In synthetic fonts, these numbers can be very different from each other. See section 9.1, "Synthetic Fonts," for more information.

After the comments, the program allocates a dictionary with a capacity of 11 elements; this dictionary will become a font dictionary. The program inserts eight items (**FontInfo**, **FontName**, **PaintType**, **FontType**, **FontMatrix**, **Encoding**, **FontBBox**, and **UniqueID**) into the dictionary. The 1000 to 1 scaling in the **FontMatrix** as shown is typical of a Type 1 font program and is highly recommended.

Also highly recommended is that the values for the **FontBBox** be as accurate as possible. The PostScript interpreter uses this information in making decisions about font caching and clipping. The **FontBBox** must be accurate (not all zeros) if the font program uses the **seac** command for creating accented characters. In this situation, an accurate **FontBBox** is critical to forming unclipped characters. If the font program does not make use of accented characters defined by the **seac** command, then **FontBBox** can consist of all zeros.

FontType *must* be set equal to 1 for all Type 1 font programs.

UniqueID is a value important to font identification and in helping the PostScript interpreter properly cache characters between jobs. **UniqueID** is discussed later in this chapter.

Next in the example program is the **Encoding** array. The **Encoding** array determines which character codes are associated with which character names in the font program. This character encoding can be changed without altering anything else in the font program.

The clear text portion of the font program is followed by an **eexec**-encrypted portion. The clear text portion ends with an invocation of the **eexec** operator, after which the font program contains ASCII hexadecimal encrypted text:

```
currentfile eexec
05f3acf73b42a65ec11a12df4c6e26
5306f37b5075f007986cdacc4cd13a
. . . thousands of eexec-encrypted bytes left out . . .
```

When **eexec** begins operation, it performs a **begin** operation on **systemdict** to ensure that the operators that follow will be taken from **systemdict**. When **eexec** terminates, it automatically performs an **end** operation to remove the **systemdict** that it begins here.

The text encrypted by **eexec** must be followed by 512 ASCII zeros. There may be white space characters (blank, tab, carriage return or line feed) interspersed among these zeros. Some zeros will be consumed by the **eexec** command; the remainder will be encountered by the PostScript interpreter and pushed onto the operand stack. A **mark** operator within the encrypted text marks the operand stack, and the final **cleartomark** operator cleans the mark and the extraneous zeros off the operand stack.

2.4 Inside the Encrypted Portion

In the encrypted portion of the font program are the **CharStrings** and the **Private** dictionaries. The **CharStrings** dictionary contains the encoded commands that draw the outlines of the characters included in the font. The **Private** dictionary contains hints and subroutines. The hints in the **Private** dictionary apply to the entire font. The **Private** dictionary may also contain various Post-Script language procedures that can modify the behavior of the font program in some versions of the PostScript interpreter. See Chapter 5, "Private Dictionary," for more information about the hinting system and Type 1 font format hints.

The character string values in the **CharStrings** dictionary must be encoded and encrypted; decrypting and decoding the string is an intrinsic part of Type 1 BuildChar. These encoded and encrypted character outline strings are called *charstrings*. When decoded, each charstring bears a resemblance to a PostScript language program, in that an operand stack and postfix syntax are used. However, the set of commands included in the charstrings is special to Type 1 BuildChar, and their operands are restricted in type and range. The operand stack for charstring operation is separate from the general PostScript language operand stack. Some commands are similar to built-in operators in the PostScript language. Other commands, such as those that give hints to the character rendering algorithm, are unique to Type 1 BuildChar's input language.

Note   *The word "encoding" is used to describe two situations in the Type 1 font format. Charstring encoding refers to the particular form of charstring contents, with commands and operands represented by short code sequences. Encoding vector refers to an assignment of character names to character codes for use in character identification to the **show** command. The meaning of the word "encoding" used in various places in this document should be clear from its context.*

By decrypting the **eexec**-encrypted portion of the Symbol font program, the following simplified code appears. In this code, a sequence of *n* binary bytes is indicated by the form *~n~binary~bytes~*.

Example 2.

```
dup /Private 8 dict dup begin
/RD {string currentfile exch readstring pop} executeonly def
/ND {noaccess def} executeonly def
/NP {noaccess put} executeonly def
/BlueValues [-17 0 487 500 673 685] def
/MinFeature {16 16} def
/password 5839 def
/UniqueID 6859 def
/Subrs 43 array
dup 0 15 RD ~15~binary~bytes~ NP
% . . .
% . . . 41 subroutine definitions omitted
% . . .
dup 42 23 RD ~23~binary~bytes~ NP
ND
2 index /CharStrings 190 dict dup begin
/Alpha 186 RD ~186~binary~bytes~ ND
% . . .
% . . . 188 character definitions omitted
% . . .
/.notdef 9 RD ~9~binary~bytes~ ND
end
end
readonly put
noaccess put
dup /FontName get exch definefont pop
mark currentfile closefile
```

Two additional items (**Private** and **CharStrings**) are added to the font dictionary. In the example font program, **Private** is associated with a dictionary of eight items, **RD**, **ND**, **NP**, **BlueValues**, **MinFeature**, **password**, **UniqueID**, and **Subrs**. **CharStrings** is associated with a dictionary of 190 items in the example; each of these items in turn associates a character name (such as **Alpha**) with an encoded and encrypted charstring. Type 1 BuildChar interprets each charstring when the character is shown for the first time. The **Subrs** entry in the **Private** dictionary contains charstring portions that can be referenced multiple times by subroutine calls from other charstrings.

Charstrings in actual Type 1 font programs use the **RD**, **ND**, and **NP** PostScript language procedures shown in the preceding example to reduce the size of the font program. In some fonts, these names might be defined in **userdict**, or they might be named -|, |-, and | respectively (constructed with hyphen and vertical bar characters) in the **Private** dictionary. Note that a character name in the **CharStrings** dictionary cannot be either **RD** or **ND** or whatever names are substituted for these names, because that would redefine these critical procedures.

While **ND** and **NP** are merely abbreviations that save some bytes of PostScript language code each time they are used, **RD** is more complicated. Each use of **RD** is followed by exactly one blank character followed by a sequence of binary bytes that are the charstring contents. This charstring is not given in ASCII hexadecimal form—it is binary. **RD** itself is preceded by an integer that tells exactly how many binary bytes follow the **RD** (not including the single blank that follows the **RD**).

Note *The **RD**, **NP**, and **ND** functions must be implemented by PostScript language procedures and must be invoked by a single name as shown in the program example. These functions may not be implemented by equivalent in-line code.*

Both the **Private** dictionary and all of the charstrings are given the **noaccess** attribute. Thus, a user of the PostScript interpreter cannot read or write their contents. This is not necessary in a Type 1 font program; it has been included in this particular example only to protect the contents of these items from casual reading. Note that while a *user* of the PostScript interpreter cannot access these items, the PostScript interpreter itself (particularly, Type 1 BuildChar) can access them.

Finally, the **definefont** operator makes the first dictionary into a font dictionary. It adds one more item, **FID**, to this font dictionary. The **mark** is provided so that the **cleartomark** operator that follows the 512 zeros can remove extra zeros from the operand stack.

The final **currentfile closefile** sequence terminates the operation of the **eexec** command. When **eexec** terminates, it automatically performs an **end** operation to remove the **systemdict** that it began.

Note *The preceding example shows a character named ".notdef" defined in the **CharStrings** dictionary. A Type 1 font program must have a ".notdef" character defined in its **CharStrings** dictionary, even if it is not referenced by the encoding vector.*

2.5 Unique Identification Numbers and Font Names

The **UniqueID** is an optional entry that helps identify the font program to the interpreter. Its primary purpose is uniquely identifying bitmaps already created and cached from that font program; having a **UniqueID** allows the PostScript interpreter to cache bitmaps across jobs.

The **UniqueID** is specified with the entry name **UniqueID** both in the font dictionary and in the **Private** dictionary. Type 1 font dictionaries presented to the **definefont** operator that differ in any way *except* in the values of **FontName**, **FontInfo**, or **Encoding** must have different **UniqueID** values. If the **UniqueID** values are not present in both the font dictionary and **Private** dictionary, or if they have different values, then the font program is treated by the interpreter as if it had no **UniqueID** at all: caching will then be efficient for the immediate job, but the interpreter will not cache bitmaps for that font across jobs.

If the **UniqueID** value in a font program is not unique, a subsequent application referencing a font program with the same **UniqueID** can inadvertently obtain bitmaps that were cached by the previous job. This is a particular problem for service bureaus where the cached characters might be written to disk and remain there during subsequent jobs.

Adobe Systems maintains a registry of **UniqueID** numbers and font names for font programs created in the Type 1 format. The **UniqueID** number is an integer in the range from 0 to 16,777,215

(2^{24}-1). Each **FontType** has its own independent space of **UniqueID** values. Therefore, a Type 1 and a Type 3 font program could have the same **UniqueID** number and be safely used together without causing caching conflicts.

The numbers from 4,000,000 to 4,999,999 form an "open" range for Type 1 font programs used in a "controlled environment." An individual, company, or service bureau can create its own font programs—such as font programs with extra characters, with logos, or with transformations—and assign numbers from the open range. ID conflicts should not occur if all other font programs in use are from vendors whose **UniqueID** numbers have been allocated by Adobe Systems.

Font vendors who plan to widely distribute Type 1 font programs should obtain a **UniqueID** number for each font program. In return for receiving **UniqueID** numbers, the vendor must agree to provide Adobe Systems with AFM (Adobe Font Metric) files for all font programs released. This is necessary to register the font name and to keep the database of font names and **UniqueID** numbers accurate and up-to-date. If you wish to obtain more information or to request **UniqueID** numbers for Type 1 font programs, please write to:

UniqueID Coordinator
Adobe Systems Incorporated
P.O. Box 7900
Mountain View, CA 94039-7900

Not all Type 1 font programs require a **UniqueID**. To determine whether a font program needs one, consider the following options:

- Published or widely-distributed font programs:
  A vendor with a Type 1 font program that will be published or distributed should obtain a **UniqueID** number assignment from Adobe Systems and register the font program's name.

- Limited-distribution or private-use font programs:
  Whether a **UniqueID** is required depends on one of two possibilities:

  1. *Controlled environment:* If the font program is going to be used only within a single department or company and the user would like bitmaps created by the font program to remain cached across subsequent jobs, insert a randomly-selected number from the "open" range in both of the dictionaries.

2. *Uncertain distribution:* If the font program is to be sent to a service bureau or if the distribution and printing environment is uncertain, Adobe encourages you *not* to use any **UniqueID** number. Within a given job, caching still performs well, but the chance of **UniqueID** conflict with other jobs is eliminated.

Type 1 font programs should also have unique names. To name a font program, use the **definefont** operator. In the example above, the value associated with **FontName** is the argument for the **definefont** operator. **definefont** takes the name and a dictionary, checks that the dictionary is a well-formed font dictionary, makes the dictionary's access read-only, and associates the font program name with the dictionary in the global dictionary **FontDirectory**. (It also inserts an additional entry whose name is **FID** and whose value is an object of type fontID; this entry serves internal purposes in the font machinery. For this reason, a font dictionary presented to **definefont** must have room for at least one additional key-value pair.)

However, while the **FontName** key in the font dictionary should be the name of the font program, it is not necessarily the name that identifies the font program to the **findfont** operator. The name supplied to the **definefont** operator is the name understood by the **findfont** operator. For this reason, Adobe Systems will also register font program names as part of the **UniqueID** number and font name data base.

CHAPTER **3**

Character Outline Considerations

Character description is the heart of any Type 1 font program. Each character shape comprises a path drawn by a series of Post-Script language programming statements. Each character in a Type 1 font can consist of no more than one such path. Of course, this one path may contain several subpaths.

3.1 Character Geography

Although there are typographic terms for a wide variety of character features, discussion here will be limited to those features relevant to Type 1 font characters and the Type 1 hinting mechanism.

The main vertical strokes of a character are generally known as vertical stems, and the horizontal strokes are known as horizontal stems. Stems can be straight or curved; see Figure 3a that follows. For example, in a Type 1 font character, the top and bottom curved strokes of an "O" can be considered horizontal stems, and the left and right sides can be considered vertical stems.

In addition to obvious stem-like features of a character, it is also important to identify serif shapes. For Type 1 hinting purposes, the serifs on an "I" are considered horizontal stems. Similarly, the vertical serifs on the cross stroke of a "T" are considered vertical stems.

Figure 3a. *Horizontal stems, vertical stems, and serifs*

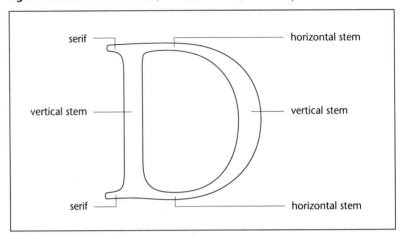

The rest of this discussion of character geography applies mainly to roman alphabet typefaces. While other alphabets (symbol sets and non-roman alphabets, such as Chinese and Arabic) share many of these features, a detailed discussion of their differences is beyond the scope of this document.

Several horizontal measurements help to define a character in the PostScript language.

- A character's *origin* is its initial reference point. The origin is made to coincide with the current point when the character is shown.

- A character's *width* is a vector, generally horizontal to the right, from the origin to the coordinate at which the current point will be set after showing this character.

- The *left sidebearing* is a vector, generally horizontal to the right, from the origin to a point whose *x* coordinate coincides with the *x* coordinate of the leftmost filled part of the character.

- The *left sidebearing point* is the coordinate at which the left sidebearing vector terminates. The *y* coordinate of the left sidebearing point is almost always 0. (There are always exceptions in font program design, and there can be conditions where the *y* coordinate of the left sidebearing point is not 0—but very few.) The first point in the defining path is measured relative to the left sidebearing point; subsequent path coordinates are measured relative to the preceding path coordinate.

Figure 3b. *Origin, width, left sidebearing and left sidebearing point*

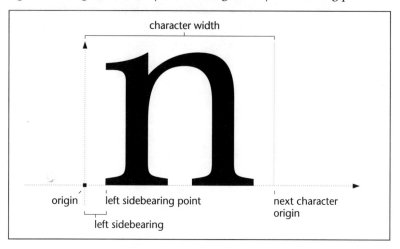

3.2 Alignments and Overshoots

Type 1 font hints include many vertical measurements that apply to an entire typeface. (Chapter 5, "Private Dictionary," describes Type 1 font hints in greater detail.) Some of these measurements help to accurately represent the slight differences in alignment between flat characters and round characters. In Type 1 font terminology, the round characters are said to *overshoot* the flat characters (at both top and bottom).

Type 1 BuildChar accepts alignment and overshoot information in pairs of numbers. One number indicates the *flat position*, or the *y* coordinate that flat characters reach; the other number is the *overshoot position*, or the *y* coordinate that curved characters reach. The pair of numbers is called an *alignment zone*. The difference between the numbers in an alignment zone is called the *alignment zone height*; this height is typically between 10 and 20 units. All coordinates in these descriptions are in character space units, and assume the 1000 to 1 character space to user space scaling that is typical of the Type 1 font format. There is one alignment zone of each type applicable across the entire font program. Several alignment zones are illustrated in Figure 3c.

- The *baseline* is the *y* coordinate of the typographic baseline of the font (the line on which most flat characters sit). The baseline is typically zero.

- The *baseline overshoot position* is the minimum y coordinate just below the baseline that round parts of characters at the baseline reach. A value of -15 is typical. Note that curved characters typically extend slightly below the baseline; as a result this value is typically negative.

- The *cap-height* is the y coordinate of the top of flat capital letters. A value of 700 is typical.

- The *cap-height overshoot position* is the maximum y coordinate just above the *cap-height* that the round parts of characters reach. A value 10 to 20 greater than *cap-height* is typical.

- The *x-height* is the y coordinate of the top of flat, non-ascending lower case letters. A value near 450 is typical.

- The *x-height overshoot position* is the maximum y coordinate just above the *x-height* that the round parts of lower case letters reach. A value 10 to 20 greater than *x-height* is typical.

Figure 3c. *Vertical measurements: baseline and baseline overshoot position, x-height and x-height overshoot position, cap-height and cap-height overshoot position*

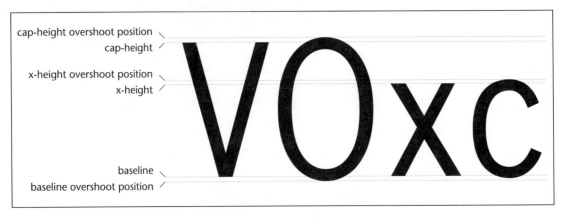

Alignment zones for the tops of character features are called *top-zones*, and alignment zones for the bottoms of character features are called *bottom-zones*. For example, the cap-height and x-height zones are top-zones, while the baseline zone is a bottom-zone. Top-zones and bottom-zones are discussed further in Chapter 5, "Private Dictionary," and Chapter 6, "CharStrings Dictionary."

Nearly all roman Type 1 font programs use baseline, cap-height and x-height alignment zones. Some of these fonts include other alignment zones as well. These zones may describe figure-height, ascender-height, descender-depth, superior baseline, ordinal baseline, and so on. The particular set of zones is chosen according to the design of the font; there is no requirement that any particular set of zones be used. For more information, see the definition of **BlueValues** in section 5.3, Chapter 5, "Private Dictionary."

3.3 Character Coordinate Space

In the PostScript language, characters have their own coordinate system distinct from the coordinate system used by a specific device. The coordinate system in which characters are defined is called *character space,* the coordinate system used by a device is called *device space*, and the coordinate system used in PostScript language programs for placing objects on a page is called *user space*.

Type 1 font programs generally use a 1000 to 1 scaling matrix for the definition of the relationship of character space units to user space units. The **FontMatrix** value in these fonts is typically [0.001 0 0 0.001 0 0]. Thus, 1000 character space units will scale down to 1 user space unit (before application of the **makefont** or **scalefont** operators in a PostScript language program). This allows character space coordinates to be expressed in integer values without significant loss of precision for most font designs. If additional precision is necessary, expressions such as 145 10 **div** may be used to provide a number (in this case, 14.5) that cannot be expressed directly in the charstring format.

Figure 3d shows how two characters are situated in the character space coordinate system. Notice that the value of 1000 is not a limit of any kind—it simply provides a coordinate system and a ratio for scaling characters to the one unit master size.

Figure 3d. *Character space coordinate system*

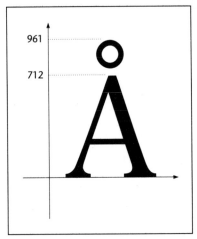 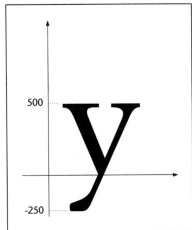

The only exceptions to the standard 1000 to 1 scaling matrix involve obliquing, narrowing, and expanding transformations applied to a font that had been originally defined by a 1000 to 1 scaling matrix. Even in these cases, at least one dimension of the **FontMatrix** will be a simple 1000 to 1 scale. Coordinates and widths should be defined for the normal 1000 to 1 scale. If a different font matrix is applied, for example, to make an oblique font from a normal font, the new font matrix will transform all these coordinates and widths together.

Type 1 BuildChar expects that the absolute coordinate values that define a character outline do not deviate too far outside of the one user space unit to which the character space coordinates will be transformed. Absolute coordinate values in both *x* and *y* directions must be between -2000 and +2000. (When coordinate values are computed using the **div** command, its *operands* may be out of this range; the final result of such a computation however, must be within this range.)

3.4 Character Paths

A character is made up of PostScript language code that draws the character in character space. The first step in preparing the contents of a charstring is to develop a PostScript language program that defines the character outline in character space. An outline is defined by building a path with the **moveto**, **lineto**, **curveto**, **closepath**, **rlineto**, etc. operators. Only characters defined by outlines may be included in Type 1 font programs; for example, the

image and **imagemask** operators are not allowed. Once the path has been expressed using only integer constants (and operations on them) for coordinates, it is a simple matter to translate from the pure PostScript language operators to the special set of commands recognized by Type 1 BuildChar. The charstring encoding allows only integers as numeric constants; however, non-integer values can be created as a result of arithmetic operations and passed to the commands. See Chapter 6, "CharStrings Dictionary," for the complete list of allowable charstring commands.

Many versions of the PostScript interpreter have an internal limit of 1500 flattened path elements per character; exceeding this bound results in a **limitcheck** error. Each character outline in a given font design must not exceed this limit when rendered. Each Type 1 font program should be tested sufficiently to verify that the font program behaves well with respect to this limit. The upper limit can be checked by testing at least the more complicated characters in a given font (the characters with the greatest number of path commands) at a reasonably large size, for example, 200 points. The characters should be tested on a high-resolution device set to its highest resolution, where flattening results in the most segments. The font should, of course, also be tested with the Adobe Type Manager software product. Kanji font characters need only be tested on Kanji printers since these printers have significantly increased limits for the number of path elements allowed.

Should a character result in a **limitcheck** error, the only choice is to try to reduce the number of path commands or to convert the font into the Type 3 font format.

Note A Type 1 font character is filled as one path; complicated characters can produce a **limitcheck** error. You must experiment to find the flattened path limit for any particular combination of device and version of the PostScript interpreter. This is why Adobe Systems encourages extensive font program testing before release. Generally, your font program either will run acceptably or it will generate a **limitcheck** error.

3.5 Direction of Paths

A subpath that is to be filled must be defined in a counterclockwise orientation in character space. A subpath that is to be left unfilled must be defined in a clockwise orientation. If you imagine walking along a subpath in the direction it is defined, then a filled area should be on your left. This convention allows Post-

Script language programs to create combinations of paths involving characters with reliable winding number orientations. On some implementations of Type 1 BuildChar, this orientation is expected; some rendering algorithms depend on it.

Figure 3e. *Construct subpaths in the correct direction*

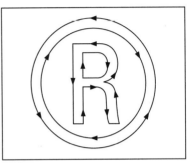

3.6 Overlapping Paths

A single closed outline should not intersect itself; this can cause winding number problems. If two filled subpaths in a character overlap, there may be no problem when the character is filled. However, a Type 1 font program can also be stroked along its outline when the user changes the **PaintType** entry in the font dictionary to 2. In this case, overlapping subpaths will be visible in the output; this yields undesirable visual results in outlined characters. Always construct the character paths with outlined output in mind.

Figure 3f. *Avoid overlapping subpaths*

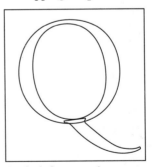

Filled character   *Stroked character: incorrect*   *Stroked character: correct*

CHAPTER 4

Technical Design Considerations

At first it may seem that character outlines need not differ much from other graphic outlines. However, the requirements of letterforms impose more stringent requirements on a character outline if it is to look good. Making a PostScript language implementation of a typeface design involves two essential considerations:

- The character paths must accurately express the true analog shapes of the original design.

- Certain conventions must be observed to help the interpreter accurately scale for all sizes.

Failure to observe either of these conventions can result in uneven stems, unwanted pixels, poor curve shapes, and poor transitions from straight to curved sections. While there are no hard and fast rules for font outline design in a Type 1 font program, paying attention to the guidelines discussed in this chapter will help ensure pleasing results.

4.1 Points at Extremes

An endpoint (first or last point of a **lineto** or **curveto**) should be placed at most horizontal or vertical extremes. This implies that most curves should not include more than 90 degrees of arc. The placement of extreme points aids the rendering algorithms in properly reproducing the major features of characters. Of course, points may be placed anywhere else on the character outline, as long as the important extremes are defined as well. It is not necessary to place an endpoint at extremes of very small curves such as the tips of curved serifs.

Figure 4a. *Place endpoints at most extremes (arrow indicates a possible exception)*

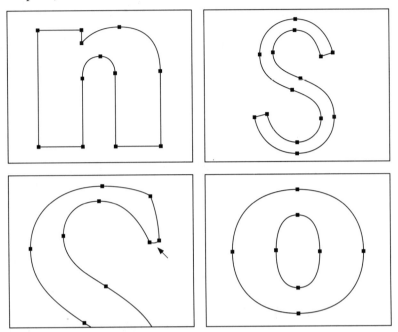

4.2 Tangent Continuity

The smooth, curved path elements that form the lines of a typeface are particularly hard to represent well when the output technology is raster-based. Tangent continuity describes the method that well-designed fonts use to produce outlines with smooth transitions.

Whenever one path element should make a smooth transition to the next element (for example, straight line to curve, curve to straight line, or curve to curve) the endpoint joining the two elements and the Bézier control points (the off-curve points) associated with that endpoint (for curves) or the other endpoint (for lines) should all be collinear. This is especially important at horizontal and vertical extremes, where slight deviations tend to be magnified by interaction with the pixel grid.

Figure 4b. *Make smooth transitions between path elements*

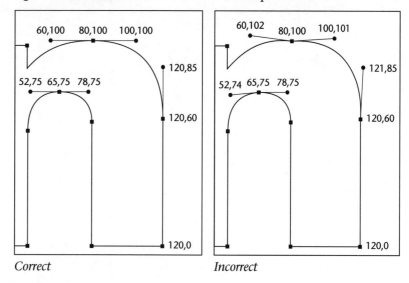

Correct   Incorrect

4.3 Conciseness

Character outline definitions should be as concise as possible, without breaking the other rules. This achieves minimum memory usage and maximum speed in the rendering system, and simplifies the task of adding hints.

- Use the fewest Bézier curve segments that accurately represent a shape.

- Do not use consecutive collinear straight line segments.

- Do not draw straight lines by using collinear **curveto** definitions (for example, "0 0 **moveto** 0 10 0 20 0 30 **curveto**").

- Whenever possible, use the **closepath** command to draw one of the straight line segments, rather than closing a character with a **closepath** that results in a zero-length line segment.

- In general, find the smallest sequence of commands that accurately describe the character shape.

Figure 4c. *Paths should be concise*

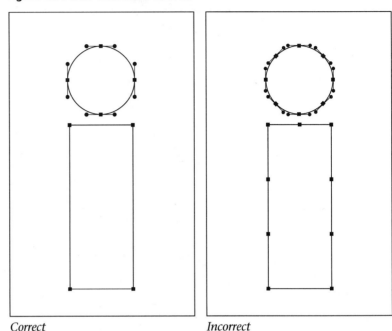

Correct   *Incorrect*

4.4 Consistency

The key to getting the best possible results is consistency. The original designs of most typefaces include many repeating weights, alignments, and shapes. Often, however, the process of creating digital outlines introduces small errors that can obscure the repeating nature of these features. Seemingly insignificant differences can become exaggerated on digital devices. Wherever possible, these errors should be eliminated.

- All stems whose widths are intended to be the same should have exactly the same width.

- All characters that are intended to align should align at exactly the same *y* coordinate.

- All shapes that are intended to be the same should be exactly the same.

- All spacing characteristics (sidebearings) that are intended to be the same should be exactly the same.

It is possible to carry consistency too far. It is important to keep in mind that Type 1 font programs are used to set type at any size on a wide range of digital devices. Type 1 font programs can be used on all PostScript language devices. The resolution and marking characteristics of these devices vary widely. They include display monitors, laser printers, typesetters, thermal transfer color printers, film recorders and many others. The resolutions range from about 75 dpi to 3000 dpi or more.

Consistency should be applied only as long as it accurately reflects the original design. Some trade-off between the results obtainable at low and high resolutions is inevitable. It is possible to achieve high quality on a particular device by adjusting the outlines to optimize for its resolution and imaging characteristics, for example, for 300-dpi write-black laser printers. However, such font software may give unsatisfactory results on devices with very different characteristics and much higher resolution. There are no requirements in the Type 1 font format that should cause font design compromises in the interests of consistency.

CHAPTER **5**

Private Dictionary

The **Private** dictionary contains hints that apply across all the characters in the font, subroutines, and several other items such as a password. Refer to Appendix 1 for a complete listing of the required and optional entries in the **Private** dictionary.

The hints used in character outlines help to preserve properties of shapes when rendered at limited resolutions. When the number of pixels in a character increases, as with very large characters or on high-resolution output devices, the hints become less important. When a stem is rendered at 100 pixels wide, a 1-pixel difference matters much less than when the stem is rendered at only 2 pixels wide. Thus, the implementation of hints mostly concerns rasterization properties at low resolutions and small sizes. With the hints in place, Type 1 BuildChar can produce results that are as close as possible to the original design even though the shape is reproduced by a relatively small number of pixels.

5.1 Declarative Hints

As with any software, there are many possible ways to design a system to compensate for low resolutions and small character sizes on a raster output device. Some methods are more efficient than others for modifying character outlines at various sizes and rotations, for requiring minimal storage, and for allowing independence from any given level of rendering technology.

Adobe Systems has created a predominantly *declarative hint system* for Type 1 font programs. Declarative hints state constraints on the size and positioning of character features, for example, the width of a stem or the location of an extremity. These declarative hints are stated in two distinct locations in a font program. The **Private** dictionary contains a number of font

35

level hints that apply across all characters represented in the font program; the individual charstrings in the **CharStrings** dictionary contain character level hints that describe important typographic features about a particular character.

A declarative hint system depends on an intelligent rasterizing algorithm to render character outlines correctly. Adobe has built such an algorithm into the PostScript interpreter and its other rendering software, such as the Adobe Type Manager program. Consequently, the appearance of font characters created with declarative hints will continue to improve as hint handling algorithms improve, without modifying the Type 1 font programs.

5.2 Font Level Hints

Hints that apply across an entire font are declared by setting certain values in the **Private** dictionary. Many of these hints declare constraints on the vertical positions of character features across the entire font. This helps to maintain consistency across the font, especially when rendered at low resolution. For historical reasons, these hints are indicated by names that contain the word "Blue."

For example, Type 1 BuildChar uses the information in the **BlueValues** and **OtherBlues** arrays to adjust the rendering of character features that fall within alignment zones. This adjustment is called *alignment control*, which at small sizes includes *overshoot suppression*. At small sizes, when only a few pixels must represent a character, a one-pixel overshoot appears too prominent.

5.3 BlueValues

The value associated with **BlueValues** is an array containing an even number of integers taken in pairs, and which follow a small number of rules:

- The first integer in each pair is less than or equal to the second integer in that pair.

- The first pair is the baseline overshoot position and the baseline. This is a bottom-zone.

- All subsequent pairs describe top-zones, that is, alignment zones for the tops of character features, for example, x-height and x-height overshoot position, ascender-height and ascender-height overshoot position, cap-height and cap-height overshoot position, figure-height and figure-height overshoot position.

- Up to seven pairs may be given in the **BlueValues** array; the first pair must be the baseline pair.

- Different pairs must be at least 3 units apart from each other and from pairs in **OtherBlues**, as described in the following section. (This minimum distance can be modified by the optional **BlueFuzz** entry in the **Private** dictionary; see the definition of **BlueFuzz**, that follows.)

- The maximum difference between values in one pair is constrained as described under the description of **BlueScale**, that follows.

For example, an array for the baseline, cap-height and x-height alignment zones in a typeface might be defined as follows:

/BlueValues [-15 0 700 715 547 559] def

Despite the names given to the various alignment zones described by the **BlueValues**, Type 1 BuildChar has no built-in notions of which parameters apply to which characters. Each zone helps to control the alignment of any and all characters with character level hints that fall within the zone.

The **BlueValues** array is required in the **Private** dictionary. If no alignment zones are necessary, use an empty array for the value of **BlueValues**:

/BlueValues [ ] def

5.4 OtherBlues

The optional **OtherBlues** entry in the **Private** dictionary is associated with an array of pairs of integers similar to the **BlueValues** array. However, the **OtherBlues** array describes bottom-zones only. For example, these may include: descender-depth overshoot position and descender-depth, superior baseline overshoot position and superior baseline, and ordinal baseline overshoot position and ordinal baseline. Up to five pairs (10 integers) may be specified in the **OtherBlues** array. Numbers in a pair must be in ascending order, with the same restriction on the maximum difference in a pair. Pairs must be at least 3 units apart from all other pairs, including those in the **BlueValues** array. (This minimum distance can be modified by the optional **BlueFuzz** entry in the **Private** dictionary.)

5.5 FamilyBlues and FamilyOtherBlues

When different styles of the same font family are mixed in text, it is often desirable to coordinate their x-heights, cap-heights, and other alignments so that they will be the same at small sizes. For example, at 72 pixels per inch, the x-height of a 10-point roman face might be 5.4 pixels while the boldface x-height might be 5.6 pixels. If the roman face is the standard for the family, Type 1 BuildChar in recent versions of the PostScript interpreter can render both faces with an x-height of 5 pixels instead of letting the boldface jump to 6 while the roman is still at 5. However, at 100 points, the roman x-height will be 54 pixels and the bold x-height will be 56.

You can include information about the dominant alignment zones in a font family so that this consistency can be enforced. When enabled, if the difference between a font's alignment and its family's standard alignment is less than 1 pixel, then Type 1 BuildChar will use the standard alignment instead of the normal alignment for that font program. Thus at 10 points in the previous example, the difference is 5.6 − 5.4 = 0.2 pixels so the standard is used. At 100 points, the difference is 56 − 54 = 2, so the specific x-height for the font is used. Family alignment values are identical to individual font alignment values; i.e., they are things like x-height, x-height overshoot, etc. The **Private** dictionary entries are as follows.

The value associated with **FamilyBlues** is an array containing an even number of integers taken in pairs. The rules governing the contents of this array are analogous to those of the **BlueValues** array.

The value associated with **FamilyOtherBlues** is an array containing an even number of integers taken in pairs. The rules governing the contents of this array are analogous to those of the **OtherBlues** array.

Typically, the **FamilyBlues** and **FamilyOtherBlues** entries will simply be copied from the **BlueValues** and **OtherBlues** of the standard face in the family. Each font program in a family (except the standard face) must have these entries if it is to have family alignment properties. Of course, if these entries are not present, then only a font program's own alignment hints will be considered.

The **FamilyBlues** and **FamilyOtherBlues** entries are relatively new additions to the Type 1 hinting system. Currently, they are interpreted by ATM software version 1.2 (and later). These features will also be recognized by future versions of the PostScript interpreter.

5.6 BlueScale

The optional **BlueScale** entry in the **Private** dictionary controls the point size at which overshoot suppression ceases. This point size varies with the number of device pixels per inch available on the device where the font program is being rendered.

- For point sizes that occupy fewer device pixels than the **BlueScale** value results in for a given device, overshoot suppression is performed. All features falling in an alignment zone are rendered at the same pixel height.

- For point sizes that occupy the same number or a greater number of device pixels than the **BlueScale** value results in, overshoot suppression is turned off, thus allowing overshoots to occur. (This behavior may be modified by the optional **BlueShift** setting; see the definition of **BlueShift**, that follows.)

The **BlueScale** value is a number directly related to the number of pixels tall that one character space unit will be before overshoot suppression is turned off. The default value of **BlueScale** is .039625, which corresponds to 10 points at 300 dpi. A simple formula that relates point size as rendered on a 300-dpi device to the **BlueScale** value is:

BlueScale = (pointsize − 0.49) ÷ 240

The formula provides a convenient number that font program designers can use to determine at what integer point size overshoot suppression should be off. However, the *exact* point size at which overshoot suppression ceases is actually 0.49 points less (at 9.51 points using the default value of **BlueScale**) than the value of *pointsize* used in the formula. Adobe recommends using the adjustment shown in the formula so that the change in overshoot suppression behavior occurs at an exact point size unlikely to be used in practice.

For example, if you wish overshoot suppression to turn off at 11 points on a 300-dpi device, you should set **BlueScale** to (11 − 0.49) ÷ 240 or 0.04379. With this one setting of **BlueScale**, overshoot suppression will turn off at proportionately smaller point sizes on higher resolution output devices or larger point sizes on lower-resolution devices such as displays. A typical **BlueScale** statement is:

/BlueScale .04379 def

Note *There is a mandatory restriction on the* ***BlueScale*** *value and the maximum height of an alignment zone that is best described in relation to the 300-dpi point size discussed above. The product of (pointsize − 0.49) × (maximum alignment zone height) must be less than 240. For example, if the maximum alignment zone height is 23 in some font program, then the overshoot suppression turnoff point size at 300 dpi can be 10 but not 11. This restriction ensures that overshoot suppression will turn off before the overshoot reaches a full device pixel.*

5.7 BlueShift

The optional **BlueShift** entry in the **Private** dictionary adds another capability to the treatment of overshoot behavior.

The value of **BlueShift** is an integer that indicates a character space distance beyond the flat position of alignment zones at which overshoot enforcement for character features occurs. The default value of **BlueShift** is 7. The single setting of **BlueShift** applies to all alignment zones, regardless of where their overshoot positions lie.

When a character's size is less than that expressed by **BlueScale**, character features that fall within alignment zones have their overshoots suppressed. For characters larger than the **BlueScale** size, character features that fall beyond the flat position of an alignment zone (above for top-zones, below for bottom-zones) by a character space distance equal to or greater than the value of **BlueShift** will overshoot, while character features closer to the flat position than the **BlueShift** value will overshoot only if their device space distance is at least one-half pixel.

The **BlueShift** value must obey a restriction if the Flex mechanism is used. For details, see section 8.3, "Flex," in Chapter 8, "Using Subroutines."

5.8 BlueFuzz

The optional **BlueFuzz** entry in the Private dictionary is an integer value that specifies the number of character space units to extend (in both directions) the effect of an alignment zone on a horizontal stem. If the top of a horizontal stem is within **BlueFuzz** units (in character space) outside of a top-zone, the interpreter will act as if the stem top were actually within the zone; the same holds for the bottoms of horizontal stems in bottom-zones. The default value of **BlueFuzz** is 1.

BlueFuzz has been a convenient means for compensating for slightly inaccurate coordinate data. The effect of a non-zero value for **BlueFuzz** can usually be better achieved by adjusting the sizes of the alignment zones. Adobe suggests that new font programs not rely on it and disable the feature by explicitly setting **BlueFuzz** to 0 in the **Private** dictionary. For example:

/BlueFuzz 0 def

Note *Because a non-zero value for **BlueFuzz** extends the range of alignment zones, alignment zones must be declared at least (2 × **BlueFuzz** + 1) units apart from each other. Therefore, a default **BlueFuzz** value of 1 implies that alignment zones should be at least 3 units apart from each other.*

5.9 Stem Width Information

There is a mechanism to tell Type 1 BuildChar about standard stem widths in a font so that Type 1 BuildChar can ensure consistency at small sizes. If a particular stem is slightly wider or narrower than standard, either by design or as a result of a small error in creating the font program, then at small sizes where a single pixel difference would be very noticeable, Type 1 Build-Char can render the stem as though it had the standard width. However, at large sizes where a single pixel difference will produce only a subtle visual effect, the stem will be allowed to deviate from the standard.

When the difference between a standard stem width and a particular stem width is small, the standard width is used. For example, if at 10 points a standard stem width corresponds to 1.4 pixels wide and a particular stem is 1.6 pixels wide, both can be rendered as a 1-pixel wide stem. However, at 100 points the standard stem would be rendered as 14 pixels wide and the particular stem would be rendered as 16 pixels wide. The information that Type 1 BuildChar needs appears in the following **Private** dictionary entries.

The entry **StdHW** is an array with only one real number entry expressing the dominant width of horizontal stems (measured vertically in character space units). For example:

/StdHW [32] def

The entry **StdVW** is an array with only one real number entry expressing the dominant width of vertical stems (measured horizontally in character space units). Typically, this will be the width of straight stems in lower case letters. (For an italic font program, give the width of the vertical stem measured at an angle perpendicular to the stem direction.) For example:

/StdVW [85] def

The entry **StemSnapH** is an array of up to 12 real numbers of the most common widths (including the dominant width given in the **StdHW** array) for horizontal stems (measured vertically). These widths must be sorted in increasing order. For example:

/StemSnapH [32 41] def

The entry **StemSnapV** is an array of up to 12 real numbers of the most common widths (including the dominant width given in the **StdVW** array) for vertical stems (measured horizontally). These widths must be sorted in increasing order. For example, you might include widths for straight and curved stems in upper and lower case letters. For an italic font, this array should be empty. For example:

/StemSnapV [85 102] def

If these stem hints are not present in the **Private** dictionary, then each stem is rendered according to its own definition (as modified by any other hints present in the font program).

The **StdHW**, **StdVW**, **StemSnapH**, and **StemSnapV** entries are relatively new additions to the Type 1 hinting system. Currently they are interpreted by ATM software version 1.2 (and later). These features will also be recognized by future versions of the PostScript interpreter.

5.10 ForceBold

At small sizes on low-resolution devices (such as display screens), features of bold characters may be rendered at only 1 pixel of thickness. Since this is the minimum thickness possible on a raster output device, normal (non-bold) characters also appear with 1-pixel wide features. If the boldness property is so important at these small sizes that bold characters should continue to appear thicker than normal characters, some Type 1 font interpreters may apply special techniques to thicken bold character features.

If the **Private** dictionary contains an entry named **ForceBold**, this behavior can be controlled explicitly. The value associated with **ForceBold** must be the Boolean value "true" or "false." If the value is "true," then in situations where character stems would normally be rendered at 1-pixel thick, a Type 1 font interpreter may thicken the stem. If the value is "false," then a Type 1 font interpreter will not perform a special thickening operation. To set **ForceBold**, use the statement:

/ForceBold true def

Adobe strongly advises font program developers to use **ForceBold** to direct font interpreters as to which bold thickening behavior is desired.

5.11 LanguageGroup

Certain groups of written languages share broad aesthetic characteristics. Identification of such language groups can prove useful for accurate character rendering.

The value of the entry **LanguageGroup** is an integer that indicates the language group of the font program. If the **Private** dictionary does not contain this entry, or if the given value is not recognized by Type 1 BuildChar, then the value of **LanguageGroup** defaults to zero. At this time, Type 1 BuildChar recognizes only two language groups, identified as group zero and group one. The future identification of other values for the **LanguageGroup** entry is reserved by Adobe Systems.

Language group 0 consists of languages that use Latin, Greek, Cyrillic, and similar alphabets. Since the value of the **LanguageGroup** entry defaults to 0, a font program corresponding to one of these languages does not need to contain this entry.

Language group 1 consists of Chinese ideographs and similar character sets, including Japanese Kanji and Korean Hangul. Font programs corresponding to one of these languages should contain the Private dictionary entry:

/LanguageGroup 1 def

For compatibility with older PostScript interpreters, creators of font programs specifying language group 1 must also include the **RndStemUp** entry in the Private dictionary:

/RndStemUp false def

The **RndStemUp** entry has been superseded by the **LanguageGroup** entry. No reference at all to the name **RndStemUp** should be made in any font program unless it belongs to language group one.

5.12 lenIV

The **lenIV** entry is an integer specifying the number of random bytes at the beginning of charstrings for charstring encryption. The default value of **lenIV** is 4.

To be compatible with version 23.0 of the PostScript interpreter (found in the original LaserWriter®), the value of **lenIV** should be set to 4. If compatibility with version 23.0 printers is not necessary, **lenIV** can be set to 0 or 1 to save storage.

5.13 Compatibility Entries

The **MinFeature** and **password** entries must be included in the **Private** dictionary to allow Type 1 BuildChar to function properly.

All Type 1 font programs should include the following assignments in the **Private** dictionary:

```
/MinFeature {16 16} def
/password 5839 def
```

5.14 ExpansionFactor

The optional **ExpansionFactor** entry is a real number that gives a limit for changing the size of a character bounding box during the processing that adjusts the sizes of counters in fonts of **LanguageGroup** 1. The default value of **ExpansionFactor** is 0.06. At small point sizes or low resolutions, the system may have to accept irregular counters rather than violate this limit. Bar code fonts or logos that need counter control may benefit by setting **LanguageGroup** to 1 and increasing the **ExpansionFactor** limit to a larger amount such as 0.5 or more. For example:

```
/ExpansionFactor 0.5 def
```

CHAPTER 6

CharStrings Dictionary

The **CharStrings** dictionary holds a collection of name-procedure pairs. The procedures to which the names refer produce the font's character outlines. Character procedures can also call subroutines (located in the **Private** dictionary) that produce similar parts of characters, thus reducing storage requirements. The charstring procedures also contain character level hints.

6.1 Charstring Encoding

A charstring is an encrypted sequence of unsigned 8-bit bytes that encode integers and commands. Type 1 BuildChar, when interpreting a charstring, will first decrypt it and then will decode its bytes one at a time in sequence. The value in a byte indicates a command, a number, or subsequent bytes that are to be interpreted in a special way.

Once the bytes are decoded into numbers and commands, the execution of these numbers and commands proceeds in a manner similar to the operation of the PostScript language. Type 1 BuildChar uses its own operand stack, called the *Type 1 Build-Char operand stack*, that is distinct from the PostScript interpreter operand stack. This stack holds up to 24 numeric entries. A number, decoded from a charstring, is pushed onto the Type 1 BuildChar operand stack. A command expects its arguments in order on this operand stack with all arguments generally taken from the bottom of the stack (first argument bottom-most); however, some commands, particularly the subroutine commands, normally work from the top of the stack. If a command returns results, they are pushed onto the Type 1 BuildChar operand stack (last result topmost).

In the following discussion, all numeric constants are decimal numbers.

6.2 Charstring Number Encoding

A charstring byte containing the values from 32 through 255 inclusive indicates an integer. These values are decoded in four ranges.

1. A charstring byte containing a value, v, between 32 and 246 inclusive, indicates the integer $v - 139$. Thus, the integer values from −107 through 107 inclusive may be encoded in a single byte.

2. A charstring byte containing a value, v, between 247 and 250 inclusive, indicates an integer involving the next byte, w, according to the formula:

$$[(v - 247) \times 256] + w + 108$$

Thus, the integer values between 108 and 1131 inclusive can be encoded in 2 bytes in this manner.

3. A charstring byte containing a value, v, between 251 and 254 inclusive, indicates an integer involving the next byte, w, according to the formula:

$$- [(v - 251) \times 256] - w - 108$$

Thus, the integer values between −1131 and −108 inclusive can be encoded in 2 bytes in this manner.

4. Finally, if the charstring byte contains the value 255, the next four bytes indicate a two's complement signed integer. The first of these four bytes contains the highest order bits, the second byte contains the next higher order bits and the fourth byte contains the lowest order bits. Thus, any 32-bit signed integer may be encoded in 5 bytes in this manner (the 255 byte plus 4 more bytes).

Note   *Numbers with absolute values greater than 32,000 must be followed by a **div** operator such that the result of the **div** is less than 32,000.*

6.3 Charstring Command Encoding

Charstring commands are encoded in 1 or 2 bytes.

Single byte commands are encoded in 1 byte that contains a value between 0 and 31 inclusive. Not all possible command encoding values are listed. The command values that are omitted are special purpose commands that are not used in any downloadable Type 1 font program, or they are reserved.

If a command byte contains the value 12, then the value in the next byte indicates a command. This "escape" mechanism allows many extra commands to be encoded. These 2-byte commands are not used as often as the 1-byte commands; this encoding technique helps to minimize the length of charstrings. Refer to Appendix 2 for a summary of the charstring commands and their encoding values.

6.4 Charstring Command List

The Type 1 font program charstring commands are divided into five groups by function:

- Commands for starting and finishing a character's outline

- Path construction commands

- Hint commands

- Arithmetic commands

- Subroutine commands

The following definitions use a format similar to that used in the *PostScript Language Reference Manual*. Parentheses following the command name either include the command value that represents this command in a charstring byte, or the two values (beginning with 12) that represent a 2-byte command.

Many commands take their arguments from the bottom-most entries in the Type 1 BuildChar stack; this behavior is indicated by the stack bottom symbol (⊢) appearing to the left of the first argument. Commands that clear the operand stack are indicated by the stack bottom symbol (⊢) in the result position of the command definition.

Because of this stack-clearing behavior, in general, operands may not be piled up on the Type 1 BuildChar operand stack for later removal by a sequence of commands. Operands generally may be supplied only for the next command. Notable exceptions occur with subroutine calls and with the **div** command.

Commands for Starting and Finishing

endchar   – **endchar** (14) ⊢

finishes a charstring outline definition and must be the last command in a character's outline (except for accented characters defined using **seac**). When **endchar** is executed, Type 1 BuildChar performs several tasks. It executes a **setcachedevice** operation, using a bounding box it computes directly from the character outline and using the width information acquired from a previous **hsbw** or **sbw** operation. (Note that this is not the same order of events as in Type 3 Fonts.) BuildChar then calls a special version of **fill** or **stroke** depending on the value of **PaintType** in the font dictionary. The Type 1 font format supports *only* **PaintType** 0 (fill) and 2 (outline). Note that this single **fill** or **stroke** implies that there can be only one path (possibly containing several subpaths) that can be created to be filled or stroked by the **endchar** command.

hsbw   ⊢ sbx wx **hsbw** (13) ⊢

sets the left sidebearing point at (*sbx*, 0) and sets the character width vector to (*wx*, 0) in character space. This command also sets the current point to (*sbx*, 0), but does not place the point in the character path. Use **rmoveto** for the first point in the path. The name **hsbw** stands for horizontal sidebearing and width; horizontal indicates that the *y* component of both the sidebearing and width is 0. Either **sbw** or **hsbw** must be used once as the first command in a character outline definition. It must be used only once. In non-marking characters, such as the space character, the left sidebearing point should be (0, 0).

seac   ⊢ asb adx ady bchar achar **seac** (12 6) ⊢

for *standard encoding accented character*, makes an accented character from two other characters in its font program. The *asb* argument is the *x* component of the left sidebearing of the accent; this value must be the same as the sidebearing value given in the **hsbw** or **sbw** command in the accent's own charstring. The origin of the accent is placed at (*adx*, *ady*) relative to the origin of the base character. The *bchar* argument is the character code of the base character, and the *achar* argument is the character code of the accent character. Both *bchar* and *achar* are codes that these characters are assigned in the Adobe StandardEncoding vector, given in an Appendix in the *PostScript Language Reference Manual*. Furthermore, the characters represented by *achar* and *bchar* must be in the same positions in the font's encoding vector as the positions they occupy in the Adobe StandardEncoding vector. If the name of both components of an accented character do not appear in the Adobe StandardEncoding vector, the accented character cannot be built using the **seac** command.

The **FontBBox** entry in the font dictionary must be large enough to accommodate both parts of the accented character. The **sbw** or **hsbw** command that begins the accented character must be the same as the corresponding command in the base character. Finally, **seac** is the last command in the charstring for the accented character because the accent and base characters' charstrings each already end with their own **endchar** commands.

The use of this command saves space in a Type 1 font program, but its use is restricted to those characters whose parts are defined in the Adobe StandardEncoding vector. In situations where use of the **seac** command is not possible, use of **Subrs** subroutines is a more general means for creating accented characters.

sbw   ⊢ sbx sby wx wy **sbw** (12 7) ⊢

sets the left sidebearing point to (*sbx, sby*) and sets the character width vector to (*wx, wy*) in character space. This command also sets the current point to (*sbx, sby*), but does not place the point in the character path. Use **rmoveto** for the first point in the path. The name **sbw** stands for sidebearing and width; the *x* and *y* components of both the left sidebearing and width must be specified. If the *y* components of both the left sidebearing and the width are 0, then the **hsbw** command should be used. Either **sbw** or **hsbw** must be used once as the first command in a character outline definition. It must be used only once.

Path Construction Commands

closepath   – **closepath** (9) ⊢

closepath closes a subpath. Adobe strongly recommends that all character subpaths end with a **closepath** command, otherwise when an outline is stroked (by setting **PaintType** equal to 2) you may get unexpected behavior where lines join. Note that, unlike the **closepath** command in the PostScript language, this command does not reposition the current point. Any subsequent **rmoveto** must be relative to the current point in force before the Type 1 font format **closepath** command was given.

Make sure that any subpath section formed by the **closepath** command intended to be zero length, is zero length. If not, the **closepath** command may cause a "spike" or "hangnail" (if the subpath doubles back onto itself) with unexpected results.

hlineto	⊢ dx **hlineto** (6) ⊢
	for *horizontal* lineto. Equivalent to *dx* 0 **rlineto**.
hmoveto	⊢ dx **hmoveto** (22) ⊢
	for *horizontal* moveto. Equivalent to *dx* 0 **rmoveto**.
hvcurveto	⊢ dx1 dx2 dy2 dy3 **hvcurveto** (31) ⊢
	for horizontal-vertical curveto. Equivalent to *dx1* 0 *dx2 dy2* 0 *dy3* **rrcurveto**. This command eliminates two arguments from an **rrcurveto** call when the first Bézier tangent is horizontal and the second Bézier tangent is vertical.
rlineto	⊢ dx dy **rlineto** (5) ⊢
	behaves like **rlineto** in the PostScript language.
rmoveto	⊢ dx dy **rmoveto** (21) ⊢
	behaves like **rmoveto** in the PostScript language.
rrcurveto	⊢ dx1 dy1 dx2 dy2 dx3 dy3 **rrcurveto** (8) ⊢
	for relative **rcurveto**. Whereas the arguments to the **rcurveto** operator in the PostScript language are all relative to the current point, the arguments to **rrcurveto** are relative to each other. Equivalent to *dx1 dy1* (*dx1+dx2*) (*dy1+dy2*) (*dx1+dx2+dx3*) (*dy1+dy2+dy3*) **rcurveto**.
vhcurveto	⊢ dy1 dx2 dy2 dx3 **vhcurveto** (30) ⊢
	for vertical-horizontal curveto. Equivalent to 0 *dy1 dx2 dy2 dx3* 0 **rrcurveto**. This command eliminates two arguments from an **rrcurveto** call when the first Bézier tangent is vertical and the second Bézier tangent is horizontal.
vlineto	⊢ dy **vlineto** (7) ⊢
	for vertical lineto. Equivalent to 0 *dy* **rlineto**.
vmoveto	⊢ dy **vmoveto** (4) ⊢
	for vertical moveto. This is equivalent to 0 *dy* **rmoveto**.

Hint Commands

dotsection	– **dotsection** (12 0) ⊢
	brackets an outline section for the dots in letters such as "i"," j", and "!". This is a hint command that indicates that a section of a charstring should be understood as describing such a feature,

rather than as part of the main outline. For more details, see section 8.2, "Dot Sections," in Chapter 8, "Using Subroutines."

hstem ⊢ y dy **hstem** (1) ⊢

declares the vertical range of a horizontal stem zone (see the following section for more information about horizontal stem hints) between the y coordinates y and $y+dy$, where y is relative to the y coordinate of the left sidebearing point. Horizontal stem zones within a set of stem hints for a single character may not overlap other horizontal stem zones. Use hint replacement to avoid stem hint overlaps. For more details on hint replacement, see section 8.1, "Changing Hints Within a Character," in Chapter 8, "Using Subroutines."

hstem3 ⊢ y0 dy0 y1 dy1 y2 dy2 **hstem3** (12 2) ⊢

declares the vertical ranges of three horizontal stem zones between the y coordinates $y0$ and $y0 + dy0$, $y1$ and $y1 + dy1$, and between $y2$ and $y2 + dy2$, where $y0$, $y1$ and $y2$ are all relative to the y coordinate of the left sidebearing point. The **hstem3** command sorts these zones by the y values to obtain the lowest, middle and highest zones, called *ymin*, *ymid* and *ymax* respectively. The corresponding dy values are called *dymin*, *dymid* and *dymax*. These stems and the counters between them will all be controlled. These coordinates must obey certain restrictions:

- *dymin = dymax*

- The distance from *ymin* + *dymin*/2 to *ymid* + *dymid*/2 must equal the distance from *ymid* + *dymid*/2 to *ymax* + *dymax*/2. In other words, the distance from the center of the bottom stem to the center of the middle stem must be the same as the distance from the center of the middle stem to the center of the top stem.

If a charstring uses an **hstem3** command in the hints for a character, the charstring must not use **hstem** commands and it must use the same **hstem3** command consistently if hint replacement is performed.

The **hstem3** command is especially suited for controlling the stems and counters of symbols with three horizontally oriented features with equal vertical widths and with equal white space between these features, such as the mathematical equivalence symbol or the division symbol.

vstem ⊢ x dx **vstem** (3) ⊢

declares the horizontal range of a vertical stem zone (see the following section for more information about vertical stem hints) between the *x* coordinates *x* and *x+dx*, where *x* is relative to the *x* coordinate of the left sidebearing point. Vertical stem zones within a set of stem hints for a single character may not overlap other vertical stem zones. Use hint replacement to avoid stem hint overlap. For more details on hint replacement, see section 8.1, "Changing Hints Within a Character," in Chapter 8, "Using Subroutines."

vstem3 ⊢ x0 dx0 x1 dx1 x2 dx2 **vstem3** (12 1) ⊢

declares the horizontal ranges of three vertical stem zones between the *x* coordinates *x0* and *x0 + dx0*, *x1* and *x1 + dx1*, and *x2* and *x2 + dx2*, where *x0*, *x1* and *x2* are all relative to the *x* coordinate of the left sidebearing point. The **vstem3** command sorts these zones by the *x* values to obtain the leftmost, middle and rightmost zones, called *xmin*, *xmid* and *xmax* respectively. The corresponding *dx* values are called *dxmin*, *dxmid* and *dxmax*. These stems and the counters between them will all be controlled. These coordinates must obey certain restrictions described as follows:

- *dxmin = dxmax*

- The distance from *xmin* + *dxmin*/2 to *xmid* + *dxmid*/2 must equal the distance from *xmid* + *dxmid*/2 to *xmax* + *dxmax*/2. In other words, the distance from the center of the left stem to the center of the middle stem must be the same as the distance from the center of the middle stem to the center of the right stem.

If a charstring uses a **vstem3** command in the hints for a character, the charstring must not use **vstem** commands and it must use the same **vstem3** command consistently if hint replacement is performed.

The **vstem3** command is especially suited for controlling the stems and counters of characters such as a lower case "m."

Arithmetic Command

div num1 num2 **div** (12 12) quotient

behaves like **div** in the PostScript language.

Subroutine Commands

callothersubr   arg1 . . . argn n othersubr# **callothersubr** (12 16) –

is a mechanism used by Type 1 BuildChar to make calls on the PostScript interpreter. Arguments *argn* through *arg1* are pushed onto the PostScript interpreter operand stack, and the PostScript language procedure in the *othersubr#* position in the **OtherSubrs** array in the **Private** dictionary (or a built-in function equivalent to this procedure) is executed. Note that the argument order will be reversed when pushed onto the PostScript interpreter operand stack. After the arguments are pushed onto the PostScript interpreter operand stack, the PostScript interpreter performs a **begin** operation on **systemdict** followed by a **begin** operation on the font dictionary prior to executing the **OtherSubrs** entry. When the **OtherSubrs** entry completes its execution, the PostScript interpreter performs two **end** operations prior to returning to Type 1 BuildChar charstring execution. Use **pop** commands to retrieve results from the PostScript operand stack back to the Type 1 BuildChar operand stack. See Chapter 8, "Using Subroutines," for details on using **callothersubr**.

callsubr   subr# **callsubr** (10) –

calls a charstring subroutine with index *subr#* from the **Subrs** array in the **Private** dictionary. Each element of the **Subrs** array is a charstring encoded and encrypted like any other charstring. Arguments pushed on the Type 1 BuildChar operand stack prior to calling the subroutine, and results pushed on this stack by the subroutine, act according to the manner in which the subroutine is coded. These subroutines are generally used to encode sequences of path commands that are repeated throughout the font program, for example, serif outline sequences. Subroutine calls may be nested 10 deep. See Chapter 8, "Using Subroutines," for other uses for subroutines, such as changing hints.

pop   – **pop** (12 17) number

removes a number from the top of the PostScript interpreter operand stack and pushes that number onto the Type 1 BuildChar operand stack. This command is used only to retrieve a result from an **OtherSubrs** procedure. For more details, see Chapter 8, "Using Subroutines."

return   – **return** (11) –

returns from a **Subrs** array charstring subroutine (that had been called with a **callsubr** command) and continues execution in the calling charstring.

setcurrentpoint ⊢ x y **setcurrentpoint** (12 33) ⊢

sets the current point in the Type 1 font format **BuildChar** to (x, y) in absolute character space coordinates without performing a charstring **moveto** command. This establishes the current point for a subsequent relative path building command. The **setcurrentpoint** command is used only in conjunction with results from **OtherSubrs** procedures.

6.5 Character Level Hints

Within a character, font program developers can add declarative hints to indicate to Type 1 BuildChar that a horizontal or vertical stem occurs between certain coordinates. These same hints are used to indicate stem-like round features, such as the leftmost, rightmost, topmost, and bottom-most parts of the letter "o". It is important to communicate to Type 1 BuildChar exactly where such features occur so that it can apply special techniques to these parts of the outline.

The **vstem** hint, for each vertical stem (such as the legs of the letter "n" or the leftmost and rightmost sections of the letter "o") takes two x values (expressed as x and *delta-x*) as arguments. These two x values indicate the horizontal range that the vertical stem's width occupies in character space. Similarly, the **hstem** hint, for each horizontal stem (such as the arms of the letter "E" or the topmost and bottom-most sections of the letter "o") takes two y values (expressed as y and *delta-y*) that indicate the vertical range that the horizontal stem's width occupies in character space. The **vstem** and **hstem** hints are called *stem hints*; they are typically the most numerous hints in a font program.

Stem hint zones of the same direction (e.g. two **hstem** hints) should not overlap each other within a character. See section 8.1, "Changing Hints Within a Character," in Chapter 8, "Using Subroutines," for a description of how to use hint replacement to avoid stem hint overlaps.

Figure 6a. *Character level stem hints (horizontal, vertical, and ghost stem hints)*

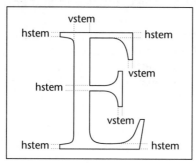
Horizontal and vertical stems

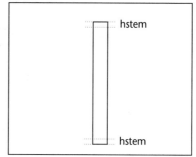
Ghost stems

Some **hstem** hints are necessary for interaction with the alignment zones declared through the **BlueValues** and **OtherBlues** hints. In order for a character's vertical features to be considered for alignment control, that character must have an **hstem** hint specified at or in an alignment zone. In some characters this happens naturally. For example, in a capital letter "E," there are at least three **hstem** hints declared for the three horizontal stems. The top stem's **hstem** hint should reach up to the cap-height, and the bottom stem's **hstem** hint should extend down to the baseline. These two **hstem** hints interact naturally with normal alignment zones.

In a sans serif capital letter "I", however, there are no horizontal stems for these **hstem** hints. In order to have the cap-height and baseline alignments apply to this character as well, the character needs **hstem** hints for non-existent horizontal stems at these positions also. These so-called "ghost" stems must be created with a stem height of 20 or 21—either is acceptable. They must describe a y coordinate range that is inside the y coordinate range of the character, not above a top nor below a bottom.

An **hstem** hint may not have its top at or in a top-zone *and* have its bottom at or in a bottom-zone. In the capital "I" example, there cannot be just one **hstem** hint that stretches from baseline to the cap-height line; instead one **hstem** should be at the cap-height and another should be at the baseline.

6.6 Encoding Example

To illustrate the composition and encoding of a charstring, consider the following example of a block letter "C". In character space this letter measures 700 units by 700 units. Its width is 800 units (horizontal), and it is centered within this width; thus its left sidebearing is 50 units wide. Each stem is 100 units wide. This example shows how to declare these stem widths as character level hints.

The charstring definition begins by writing an outline in the PostScript language in character space integer coordinates:

```
50 0 moveto 700 0 rlineto 0 100 rlineto -600 0 rlineto
0 500 rlineto 600 0 rlineto 0 100 rlineto -700 0 rlineto
closepath
```

Next, add sidebearing, width and hint information. Since the **moveto** command is not in the charstring command set, change it to **rmoveto**, taking advantage of the **hsbw** command's setting of Type 1 BuildChar's current point. Note that the **vstem** and **hstem** arguments are relative to the left sidebearing point.

```
50 800 hsbw 0 100 vstem 0 100 hstem 600 100 hstem
0 0 rmoveto 700 0 rlineto 0 100 rlineto -600 0 rlineto
0 500 rlineto 600 0 rlineto 0 100 rlineto -700 0 rlineto
closepath
```

The initial **rmoveto** command (or its equivalent) is required, as the **hsbw** command only sets the current point but does not actually place that point in the character path. In this example, the first point on the path is the same as the left sidebearing point, thus the two zero arguments to the **rmoveto** command. In other character outlines, the initial **rmoveto** point need not be the same as the left sidebearing point.

Note that there are many horizontal and vertical **rlineto** commands. Modify them to **hlineto** and **vlineto** commands for space efficiency. Finish the character with an **endchar** command.

```
50 800 hsbw 0 100 vstem 0 100 hstem 600 100 hstem
0 hmoveto 700 hlineto 100 vlineto -600 hlineto
500 vlineto 600 hlineto 100 vlineto -700 hlineto
closepath endchar
```

Encode the integers according to charstring number encoding:

189 249 180 hsbw 139 239 vstem 139 239 hstem 248 236 239 hstem
139 hmoveto 249 80 hlineto 239 vlineto 252 236 hlineto
248 136 vlineto 248 236 hlineto 239 vlineto 253 80 hlineto
closepath endchar

Encode the commands according to charstring command encoding:

189 249 180 13 139 239 3 139 239 1 248 236 239 1
139 22 249 80 6 239 7 252 236 6
248 136 7 248 236 6 239 7 253 80 6
9 14

For purposes of illustrating this example, this sequence of numbers is rewritten in ASCII hexadecimal, and shown as a sequence of PostScript language code:

```
/C <BDF9B40D8BEF038BEF01F8ECEF01
    8B16F95006EF07FCEC06
    F88807F8EC06EF07FD5006
    090E> def
```

All that remains is to apply charstring encryption to this hexadecimal-encoded binary string, and this charstring is complete.

Remember that the actual format required by Type 1 BuildChar is not this ASCII hexadecimal form of charstring, but the binary form of the charstring in the following manner:

```
/C 37 RD ~37~binary~bytes~ ND
```

CHAPTER 7

Encryption

Type 1 font programs incorporate two types of encryption: charstring encryption and **eexec** encryption.

The encoded charstrings are encrypted first. This level of encryption is called *charstring encryption*; Type 1 BuildChar works only with encoded and encrypted charstrings. A section of the Type 1 font program, including the **Private** and **CharStrings** dictionaries, is again encrypted using another layer of encryption called *eexec encryption*. This layer of encryption is intended to protect some of the hint information in the **Private** dictionary from casual inspection, and it coincidentally provides an ASCII hexadecimal form of this part of the font program so that it can be passed through communication channels that accept only 7-bit ASCII.

7.1 Encryption Method

Both **eexec** and charstring encryption employ the same encryption method. This method is a combination of three techniques.

- A pseudo-random number generator generates a sequence of keys that are combined with the plaintext to produce the ciphertext.

- Cipher feedback is employed in the generation of these keys; in other words, each byte of ciphertext is used in the production of the next key.

- Each plaintext sequence has a semi-random sequence of bytes inserted at the beginning, so that repeated encryption of the same plaintext will produce different ciphertexts.

The following algorithms for encryption and decryption are nearly identical, but they differ subtly because it is always the ciphertext byte that is used to generate the next key. It is necessary to use two separate procedures to handle encryption and decryption.

To Encrypt a Sequence of Plaintext Bytes to Produce a Sequence of Ciphertext Bytes

1. Generate n random bytes to be additional plaintext bytes at the beginning of the sequence of plaintext bytes, for some value of n.

2. Initialize an unsigned 16-bit integer variable R to the encryption key.

3. For each 8-bit byte, P, of plaintext (beginning with the newly added random bytes) execute the following steps:

   a. Assign the high order 8 bits of R to a temporary variable, T.

   b. Exclusive-OR P with T, producing a ciphertext byte, C.

   c. Compute the next value of R by the formula $((C + R) \times c1 + c2)$ mod 65536, where $c1$ is 52845 (decimal) and $c2$ is 22719 (decimal).

This encryption step can be performed by the following C language program, where r is initialized to the key for the encryption type:

```
unsigned short int r;
unsigned short int c1 = 52845;
unsigned short int c2 = 22719;

unsigned char Encrypt(plain) unsigned char plain;
{unsigned char cipher;
cipher = (plain ^ (r>>8));
r = (cipher + r) * c1 + c2;
return cipher;
}
```

To Decrypt a Sequence of Ciphertext Bytes to Produce the Original Sequence of Plaintext Bytes

1. Initialize an unsigned 16-bit integer variable R to the encryption key (the same key as used to encrypt).

2. For each 8-bit byte, C, of ciphertext the following steps are executed:

   a. Assign the high order 8 bits of R to a temporary variable, T.

   b. Exclusive-OR C with T, producing a plaintext byte, P.

   c. Compute the next value of R by the formula $((C + R) \times c1 + c2) \bmod 65536$, where $c1$ and $c2$ are the same constants that were used to encrypt.

3. Discard the first n bytes of plaintext; these are the random bytes added during encryption. The remainder of the plaintext bytes are the original sequence.

The decryption step can be performed by the following C language program, where r is initialized to the key for the encryption type:

```
unsigned short int r;
unsigned short int c1 = 52845;
unsigned short int c2 = 22719;

unsigned char Decrypt(cipher) unsigned char cipher;
{unsigned char plain;
plain = (cipher ^ (r>>8));
r = (cipher + r) * c1 + c2;
return plain;
}
```

7.2 eexec Encryption

In **eexec** encryption, the initial key for the variable R is 55665 (decimal). The number of random bytes, n, is 4.

The **eexec** operator is capable of decrypting input in either binary or ASCII hexadecimal form. There are several restrictions:

- To distinguish between binary and ASCII hexadecimal input, the first 4 ciphertext bytes must obey certain restrictions. Remember that two ASCII hexadecimal characters represent 1 ciphertext byte, while 1 binary byte represents 1 ciphertext byte.

- The first ciphertext byte must not be an ASCII white space character code (blank, tab, carriage return or line feed).

- At least one of the first 4 ciphertext bytes must not be one of the ASCII hexadecimal character codes (a code for 0-9, A-F, or a-f). These restrictions can be satisfied by adjusting the initial random plaintext bytes as necessary.

If the **eexec**-encrypted text is supplied in binary form, then every byte is considered part of the ciphertext. If the **eexec**-encrypted text is supplied in ASCII hexadecimal form, then ASCII white space characters (blank, tab, carriage return and line feed) may be freely interspersed within the encrypted text, except in the first eight characters.

Note   *It is possible not to use **eexec** encryption; however, part of the file would then be in binary, and might cause difficulty when transferring the font program over a communications line.*

7.3 Charstring Encryption

In charstring encryption, the initial key for the variable R is 4330 (decimal). The number of random bytes, n, is set within the font. By default, n is 4. However, if an entry name **lenIV** is present in the **Private** dictionary, then n is the value associated with **lenIV**. (Version 23.0 of the PostScript interpreter requires n to be 4.)

Unlike **eexec** encryption, charstring encryption imposes no restrictions on the values of the initial ciphertext bytes.

A continuation of the encoding example in section 6.6 shows how the charstring can be encrypted. Recall that the charstring looked like

```
BDF9B40D8BEF038BEF01F8ECEF018B16F9
5006EF07FCEC06F88807F8EC06EF07FD5006090E
```

in ASCII hexadecimal notation. These 74 ASCII hexadecimal characters represent 37 plaintext bytes of charstring. Generate four random plaintext bytes to insert at the front of this plaintext charstring. This example uses four zeros (for ease of explanation), resulting in this plaintext:

```
00000000BDF9B40D8BEF038BEF01F8ECEF018B16F9
5006EF07FCEC06F88807F8EC06EF07FD5006090E
```

Apply charstring encryption to produce the following 41 bytes of ciphertext expressed in ASCII hexadecimal:

10BF31704FAB5B1F03F9B68B1F39A66521B1841F14
81697F8E12B7F7DDD6E3D7248D965B1CD45E2114

When this encoded and encrypted charstring is expressed in binary form, it is ready for inclusion in a Type 1 font program. The charstring would be inserted in the **CharStrings** dictionary as follows:

/C 41 RD ~41~binary~bytes~ ND

If **eexec** encryption is to be used, it still remains to be applied over the whole of the **Private** and **CharStrings** dictionaries. This example does not show this additional encryption step.

CHAPTER **8**

Using Subroutines

A Type 1 font program uses two arrays of subroutines, **Subrs** and **OtherSubrs**. Uses for subroutines include:

- Reducing the storage requirements of a font program by combining the program statements that describe common elements of the characters in the font.

- **Subrs** 0 through 2 work with the Flex feature.

- **Subrs** 3 works with hint replacement.

- **Subrs** 4 and higher work with charstring calls.

- **OtherSubrs** 0 through 2 implement the Flex feature.

- **OtherSubrs** 3 implements hint replacement.

The **Subrs** array contains sections of outlines encoded and encrypted as charstrings, and, when hint replacement is required, sequences of stem hint commands. When a font contains repeated elements, such as serifs, equal sized bowls, and so forth, they may be candidates for charstring subroutines.

Note that the charstring command set includes only relative forms of path building commands. For example, **rmoveto** and **rlineto** are included, but **moveto** and **lineto** are not. Using relative motion commands facilitates the reuse of subroutines for sections of character outlines, regardless of their absolute placement within the character.

An element of the **Subrs** array is a charstring, encoded and encrypted separately in the same way as charstrings in the **CharStrings** dictionary. A charstring subroutine must end with the **return** command. These subroutines are called with the

callsubr command, using the index in the **Subrs** array as the argument. Charstring subroutines may call other subroutines, to a depth of 10 calls.

Using charstring subroutines is not a requirement of a Type 1 font program. However, their use contributes greatly to reducing storage space.

The Adobe® Type Library uses the **OtherSubrs** mechanism for the hint replacement function and the Flex function. These **OtherSubrs** procedures work by using some coordinated **Subrs** entries as well. All Adobe Type 1 font programs that use these functions use them in precisely the same way. As a result, the semantics of the PostScript language procedures included in the **OtherSubrs** array have stabilized to the point where the first four **OtherSubrs** entries and the first four **Subrs** entries have fixed meanings. Some Type 1 font rasterization programs such as the Adobe Type Manager software product ignore the PostScript language definitions of the **OtherSubrs** entries, choosing internal code for the particular functions according to the entry number. However, in order to work with the Type 1 BuildChar in PostScript interpreters, some PostScript language implementation of the **OtherSubrs** entries must be included in any Type 1 font program that uses these functions. The PostScript language code used in Adobe Type 1 font programs is listed in Appendix 3, "OtherSubrs Programs."

OtherSubrs entries beyond the first four are reserved for future extensions. Each new **OtherSubrs** entry will be designed so that it can be safely treated by an interpreter that does not understand its semantics. However, the first four **OtherSubrs** entries cannot be so ignored; ignoring them will result in improper execution of the charstring.

An **OtherSubrs** entry is invoked by the **callothersubr** command. This command takes (from the top of the Type 1 BuildChar operand stack down) the index number of the **OtherSubrs** entry, the number of arguments that entry expects, and the actual numeric arguments.

The complete calling sequence for an **OtherSubrs** procedure is:

arg1 arg2 . . . argn n othersubr# callothersubr pop . . . pop

The **pop** commands following the subroutine call transfer results from the PostScript operand stack to the Type 1 BuildChar operand stack. The number of **pop** commands following the call may not exceed the number of arguments, *n*. The **pop** commands, if any, must immediately follow the **callothersubr** command with no intervening commands.

If the entry number, *othersubr#*, is not one that a Type 1 font interpreter recognizes, then the results for the **pop** commands must be taken from the arguments. In this case, the first **pop** command receives *arg1*, the second **pop** command receives *arg2*, etc., with extra arguments discarded. If the Type 1 font interpreter has access to a PostScript language interpreter, it can invoke the **OtherSubrs** entry with the arguments as described under the **callothersubr** command, and the **pop** commands, if any, receive their values from the PostScript operand stack. In any case, the first four **OtherSubrs** entries must be handled according to their semantics as defined in this document.

8.1 Changing Hints Within a Character

The stem hints, **vstem** and **hstem**, affect the treatment of all subsequent coordinates in a charstring. Occasionally a character outline may require certain stem hints for some part of its outline, but different stem hints for other parts of its outline. After executing the coordinate commands for the current set of stem hints, these hints may be discarded and new stem hints given in mid-outline.

To discard old stem hints and insert new ones, the new stem hints must be placed in a charstring subroutine in the **Subrs** array. This subroutine may be placed at any index in the **Subrs** array except 0 through 3. Call this subroutine index *subr#*. This subroutine must contain only stem hint commands and their arguments. Then, at the point in the character outline where the old hints are discarded and the new ones inserted, insert the following charstring sequence:

subr# 1 3 callothersubr pop callsubr

This sequence of code operates as follows. Entry 3 in the **OtherSubrs** array is called with one argument, the entry in the **Subrs** array that contains the new hint commands. The *subr#* is pushed onto the PostScript interpreter operand stack, and the PostScript interpreter executes the hint-changing procedure. The earliest versions of the PostScript interpreter are not capable of dis-carding hints in mid-outline, so the hint-changing procedure checks if the PostScript interpreter is capable of performing this action. If so, it leaves *subr#* on the PostScript interpreter operand stack. If not, it removes *subr#* and it pushes the number 3 on the operand stack. Back in the charstring, the **pop** command transfers the number (either 3 or *subr#*) from the PostScript interpreter operand stack to the Type 1 BuildChar operand stack. Finally this subroutine is called by the **callsubr** command.

Entry 3 in the **Subrs** array is a charstring that does nothing. If the Type 1 BuildChar version is not capable of discarding old hints in mid-outline, then this mechanism ignores the new hints.

In charstring encoding (decimal) the above code sequence (with the encoding of *subr#* shown as *enc(subr#)*) is:

enc(subr#) 140 142 12 16 12 17 10

Figure 8a. *Changing hints within a character definition*

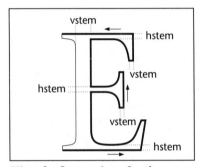 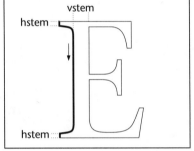

Hints for first portion of path   *Hints for second portion of path*

Specifically, for the "E" shown in Figure 8a, the charstring definition would consist of the charstring commands in the following example. Note where hint replacement is performed because of the overlapping **hstem** hints for the serifs and stems. (The stem hints for the serifs are narrower than those for the stems.)

Example 1.

40 575 hsbw	*Set left sidebearing point and width*
0 32 hstem	*Stem hint for bottom stem*
350 32 hstem	*Stem hint for middle stem*
668 32 hstem	*Stem hint for top stem*
421 36 vstem	*Stem hint for top vertical serif*
359 26 vstem	*Stem hint for middle vertical serif*
86 97 vstem	*Stem hint for main vertical stem*
0 hmoveto	*Move to first point in character path*
% ...commands omitted...	*Define first portion of character path*
4 1 3 callothersubr pop callsubr	*Change hints*
% ...commands omitted...	*Define second portion of character path with new hints in place*
closepath	*Close character path*
endchar	*End charstring outline definition*

Subroutine index number 4 in the **Subrs** array contains the following charstring sequence for defining new stem hints:

0 26 hstem	*Stem hint for bottom serif*
674 26 hstem	*Stem hint for top serif*
86 97 vstem	*Stem hint for main vertical stem*
return	*Return to charstring execution*

8.2 Dot Sections

In older PostScript interpreters not capable of performing hint replacement, a special feature was employed for dot sections of a character outline. These dot sections occur in letters such as "i", "j", and "!". Occasionally, the hints for character stems and alignment zones would interact poorly with these dots. Today, these features are best handled by hint replacement as described above. However, for compatibility with older PostScript interpreters and older Type 1 font programs, the **dotsection** hint remains available, and current font programs still use **dotsection** for compatibility with the oldest PostScript interpreters.

The **dotsection** hint command must be used in pairs at particular places in the charstring. The first **dotsection** command should occur immediately after the first **rmoveto** that begins the dot section of a character. The second **dotsection** command should be given immediately after the **closepath** that finishes the dot.

Here is an example of how **dotsection** commands should be placed in a command sequence. This dot section sequence consists of four **rrcurveto** commands:

```
. . . 0 120 rmoveto dotsection
0 -55 45 -45 55 0 rrcurveto 55 0 45 45 0 55 rrcurveto
0 55 -45 45 -55 0 rrcurveto -55 0 -45 -45 0 -55 rrcurveto
closepath dotsection . . .
```

8.3 Flex

Very shallow curves that are nearly horizontal or nearly vertical in orientation are especially difficult to approximate on a digital device. Examples of such curves include cupped serifs and tapered stems. These features can be controlled with the Flex mechanism, which uses **OtherSubrs** entries 0, 1, and 2.

The main idea behind Flex is that at small sizes slight humps and dents in an outline should disappear, while at larger sizes they should appear. Without Flex, a hump or a dent will be rendered proportionately too large at small sizes to look right. These features should appear when the subtle effect expected can be rendered appropriately.

A particular curve sequence is a candidate for Flex only if the arrangement of points on that curve meets certain conditions.

- The sequence must be formed by exactly two Bézier curve segments.

- The outer endpoints must be at the same x (or y) coordinate; in other words, they must be precisely vertical or horizontal.

- The joining endpoint between the two curves and the control points associated with this endpoint must all be positioned at the horizontal (or vertical) extreme of the double curve section. The joining point need not be equidistant from the endpoints of the double curve section.

- The difference in x (or y) coordinates between an outer endpoint and the center (joining) endpoint (the *flex height*) must be 20 units or less.

Figure 8b. *Appropriate and inappropriate curves for the Flex mechanism*

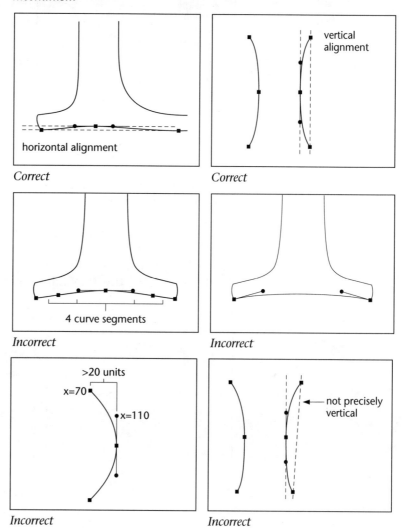

Correct   *Correct*

Incorrect   *Incorrect*

Incorrect   *Incorrect*

For best results on cupped serifs (and any other shallow curves that lie within an alignment zone), the joining (center) endpoint should be positioned precisely at the "flat" edge of the alignment zone.

Figure 8c. *Position joining endpoint at flat edge of alignment zone*

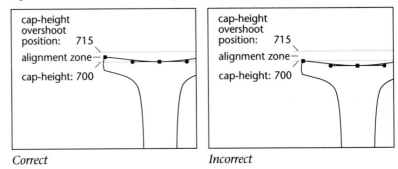

Correct   *Incorrect*

Flex features must be coordinated with the **Private** dictionary **BlueShift** value. The **BlueShift** value must be larger than the maximum Flex feature height. Since the default value of **BlueShift** is 7, this entry must be set explicitly if the maximum Flex feature height is more than 6. For example, if the maximum Flex feature height is 8, then set **BlueShift** to 9. If the maximum Flex feature height is 6 or less, the **BlueShift** entry may be omitted.

Figure 8d. *Set BlueShift value to maximum Flex feature height plus 1*

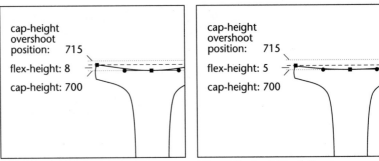

BlueShift *value set to 9*   **BlueShift** *should be left out*

The Flex mechanism chooses whether the two Bézier curves should be used as defined, or whether a straight line segment between the two outer endpoints should be used instead. The method calculates whether the height of the Flex feature in device space is less than a height control parameter. If so, then the two curves are replaced by a single straight line segment. If not, the curve points are adjusted so that the curve features will be rendered appropriately.

To encode two Bézier curve segments for Flex, several changes must be made in the charstring. The following is an algorithm that accomplishes these changes.

1. Note the coordinates of the current point in character space where the first curve begins. Call this the starting point.

2. Compute the relative distance from the starting point to a reference point. For horizontally oriented curves, the reference point will have the same x coordinate as the joining point and the same y coordinate as the starting point. For vertically oriented curves, the reference point will have the same y coordinate as the joining point and the same x coordinate as the starting point.

3. Remove the two **rrcurveto** commands, leaving six coordinate values (12 numbers).

4. Recompute the coordinates of the first pair to be relative to the reference point.

5. Insert at the beginning of the sequence the coordinate of the reference point relative to the starting point. There are now seven coordinate values (14 numbers) in the sequence.

6. Place a call to **Subrs** entry 1 at the beginning of this sequence of coordinates, and place an **rmoveto** command and a call to **Subrs** entry 2 after each of the seven coordinate pairs in the sequence.

7. Place the Flex height control parameter and the final coordinate expressed in absolute terms (in character space) followed by a call to **Subrs** entry 0 at the end.

Figure 8e. *Calculating Flex*

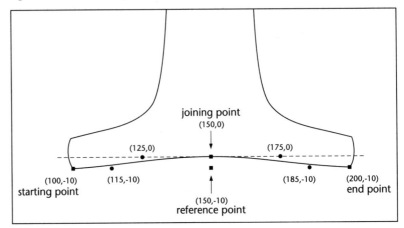

For example, consider a section of PostScript code that defines two Bézier curves that meet the requirements for Flex. See Figure 8e. This outline section begins at the point (100, -10) (in absolute character space; relative to the character space origin) and is to be included in a font whose baseline is at zero.

```
100 -10 moveto
115 -10 125 0 150 0 curveto
175 0 185 -10 200 -10 curveto
```

The Flex height is 10, the control points closest to the center end-point are at the same y coordinate, and the two endpoints are at the same y coordinate. Thus, this sequence of two curves begins at (100, -10), joins at (150, 0) and ends at (200, -10). Furthermore, the joining coordinate is at the same y coordinate as the baseline.

This outline fragment can be expressed with **rrcurveto** commands suitable for inclusion in a charstring as follows:

```
15 0 10 10 25 0 rrcurveto
25 0 10 -10 15 0 rrcurveto
```

To convert this charstring fragment to the Flex form, remove the **rrcurveto** commands and recompute the coordinates of the first pair to be relative to the reference point (150, -10):

```
-35 0 10 10 25 0 25 0 10 -10 15 0
```

Insert the coordinate of the reference point, relative to the starting point, at the beginning of this sequence and start with a call to the Subrs entry 1:

```
1 callsubr 50 0 -35 0 10 10 25 0 25 0 10 -10 15 0
```

Add the **rmoveto** commands and calls to **Subrs** entry 2:

```
1 callsubr
50 0 rmoveto 2 callsubr
-35 0 rmoveto 2 callsubr
10 10 rmoveto 2 callsubr
25 0 rmoveto 2 callsubr
25 0 rmoveto 2 callsubr
10 -10 rmoveto 2 callsubr
15 0 rmoveto 2 callsubr
```

Add the final parameters and call to **Subrs** entry 0. The first number declares the size (in hundredths of a device unit) of the rendered Flex height at which the two curves will be expressed as curves rather than as a straight line. For cupped serifs or other features that interact with overshoot zones, 50 (or one-half of a device pixel) should be used for this control parameter. Thus, if the Flex height renders to 50 hundredths of a pixel or more, the curves will be used; if less, a straight line will be used. The second and third numbers are the final coordinate expressed in absolute terms in character space (relative to the character space origin). In this example, they are 200 and -10:

```
1 callsubr
50 0 rmoveto 2 callsubr
-35 0 rmoveto 2 callsubr
10 10 rmoveto 2 callsubr
25 0 rmoveto 2 callsubr
25 0 rmoveto 2 callsubr
10 -10 rmoveto 2 callsubr
15 0 rmoveto 2 callsubr
50 200 -10 0 callsubr
```

In this example, the Flex feature height is 10. If this is the maximum Flex feature height for the entire font, then the value of **BlueShift** should be set to 11.

8.4 First Four Subrs Entries

If Flex or hint replacement is used in a Type 1 font program, the first four entries in the **Subrs** array in the **Private** dictionary must be assigned charstrings that correspond to the following code sequences. If neither Flex nor hint replacement is used in the font program, then this requirement is removed, and the first **Subrs** entry may be a normal charstring subroutine sequence. The first four **Subrs** entries contain:

Subrs entry number 0:

3 0 callothersubr pop pop setcurrentpoint return

Subrs entry number 1:

0 1 callothersubr return

Subrs entry number 2:

0 2 callothersubr return

Subrs entry number 3:

return

These code sequences must be encoded and encrypted via charstring encryption in accordance with the rest of the font program. They must then be included in the program using the **RD–NP** format.

The **Subrs** entries 1 and 2 are merely abbreviations for calling **OtherSubrs** entries. This saves two charstring bytes on each call. **Subrs** entry 3 does nothing; it is used when Type 1 BuildChar cannot perform hint replacement. **Subrs** entry 0 passes the final three arguments in the Flex mechanism into **OtherSubrs** entry 0. That procedure puts the new current point on top of the Post-Script interpreter operand stack. **Subrs** entry 0 then transfers these two coordinate values to the Type 1 BuildChar operand stack with two **pop** commands and makes them the current point coordinates with a **setcurrentpoint** command.

CHAPTER 9

Special Font Organizations

Because Type 1 fonts are PostScript language programs, their contents have sometimes been arranged in more complicated ways than already described. This chapter describes two special forms that have been used in Adobe Type 1 font programs: synthetic and hybrid fonts. Type 1 font parsers must be able to recognize these forms correctly. This chapter is intended primarily for people who are parsing an existing Type 1 font program and rendering it.

9.1 Synthetic Fonts

A *synthetic font* is a font program that is a modification of another font program by means of a different transformation matrix. Obliqued, expanded, and condensed fonts are examples of fonts that may be constructed as synthetic fonts. True italic faces and high-quality compressed and expanded faces should have completely new character outlines. However, a synthetic font program may sometimes work almost as well, at typically large savings in PostScript interpreter VM usage.

A synthetic font program associates its **CharStrings** dictionary entry with the **CharStrings** dictionary from a font program already loaded in the PostScript interpreter's VM. Thus, the additional storage required for the synthetic font program is only for its font dictionary; the large **CharStrings** dictionary is shared with the "basic" font program. A synthetic font program needs its own **UniqueID** number, so it must construct its own **Private** dictionary. This dictionary must be a clone of the basic font's **Private** dictionary except for the **UniqueID** entry.

Practically, however, there is no guarantee that the basic font program for a particular synthetic font will actually be in VM when the synthetic font is loaded. Thus, a synthetic font must contain a copy of the basic font program. The algorithm contained in PostScript language code in the synthetic font program checks for the existence of the basic font program in the **FontDirectory** dictionary in the PostScript interpreter. It also checks to see that the basic font has a **FontType** equal to one, and if the **UniqueID** is known, that it is the same as that of the synthetic font. If these conditions are met, then the synthetic font proceeds to discard the basic font it contains (by using **readstring** on itself), and it copies the **CharStrings** dictionary from the pre-existing basic font program. If the basic font program doesn't exist, then the synthetic font program executes the basic font it contains and constructs itself as before. In this second case, two font dictionaries, the basic font and the synthetic font, are created in VM rather than only the synthetic font being created.

The method for checking whether a basic font dictionary exists uses the **known** operator on the **FontDirectory** dictionary. A synthetic font program must use the token "FontDirectory" after the first occurrence of the token "/Private". This first occurrence will take place where the synthetic font program defines its **Private** dictionary, not where the embedded basic font program defines its **Private** dictionary.

9.2 Hybrid Fonts

A *hybrid font* is a font program that contains two sets of outlines. One set of outlines is chosen according to the resolution of the device on which the font is being used. Hybrid font programs are typically used for typeface designs with subtle curves that are beyond the Flex mechanism's capabilities. At high resolutions a set of outlines with full fidelity to the design is used; at low resolutions a set of outlines with straighter edges is used. An example of a hybrid font program in the Adobe Type Library is Optima*.

In a hybrid font program, the **Subrs** entries and the **CharStrings** entries occur several times. All the **Subrs** entries for the set of outlines intended for low-resolution rendering occur in a group as in a normal Type 1 font program; these are followed by all the **Subrs** entries for high-resolution rendering. These groups are separated by PostScript language code that checks resolution and that ignores one of the groups by means of **save** and **restore** operators. The **CharStrings** entries (which occur last in the font program as always), are grouped and selected in the same way.

The PostScript language code that checks the resolution of the output device sets a value in an identifier named **hires**. If the token "hires" occurs in a Type 1 font program prior to the first occurrence of "/Subrs", it must be a hybrid font program in the form described above.

CHAPTER 10

Adobe Type Manager Compatibility

There are Type 1 font program interpreters, such as in Adobe Type Manager software, that do not incorporate a complete PostScript interpreter. This kind of Type 1 font rendering software parses the Type 1 font program in a particularly simple fashion. Type 1 fonts must strictly conform to these parsing rules in addition to being legal PostScript language programs. The example font program shown in Chapter 2, "Font Program Organization," exhibits the properties that a Type 1 font program must have.

Simplified parsers can separate the input text of a Type 1 font program into tokens according to PostScript language rules as defined in the *PostScript Language Reference Manual*. (Comments and binary contents of charstrings are ignored when looking for tokens.) Simplified parsers can check tokens occurring at "top level" (not contained within procedure bodies) for certain keywords, then take specific actions based on those keywords.

- Individual tokens and charstrings may not exceed 65,535 characters in length.

- Most keywords are names that are associated with values in a dictionary; the initial portion of a Type 1 font program is assumed to contain names to be inserted in the font dictionary.

- If the keyword **eexec** appears, then the text following must be encrypted. No assignments of values to names may occur in the plaintext that follows the encrypted portion.

- All font dictionary assignments (except for **CharStrings** and **Private**) must take place before the first occurrence of the keyword /**Private**.

- All assignments following **/Private** (except for **CharStrings** contents) must be in the **Private** dictionary.

- If the **eexec** operator is used, it must occur before the first occurrence of the token **/Private**. **eexec** is not a part of the PostScript language, but is an additional operator understood by the PostScript interpreter, whose purpose is to execute encrypted font code.

10.1 Simple Values

When a simple value (integer, real, string, name, or Boolean) is associated with a name in a dictionary, that value must follow the name immediately as the next token.

Boolean values may only be the tokens **true** or **false**. Simple values, such as integers, must be written explicitly following a name; they may not be computed by a sequence of PostScript language constants and operators.

For example,

/FontType 1 def

follows the correct pattern, but

1 /FontType exch def

and

/FontType 2 1 sub def

do not conform to Type 1 font parsing rules even though they are legal and equivalent PostScript language code.

10.2 Arrays

When an array is expected as a value, the array must immediately follow the name to which it is assigned. An array must begin with either [or { and terminate with the corresponding] or }. Numeric contents must occur as single tokens within the array delimiters.

10.3 Keywords

Values for certain keywords must conform to their own rules as described as follows:

- The tokens following /**Encoding** may be **StandardEncoding def**, in which case the Adobe Standard Encoding will be assigned to this font program. For special encodings, assignments must be performed as shown in the example in section 2.3, "Explanation of a Typical Font Program," using the repetitive sequence:

  dup *index charactername* put

  where *index* is an integer corresponding to an entry in the **Encoding** vector, and *charactername* refers to a PostScript language name token, such as /**Alpha** or /**A**, giving the character name assigned to a particular character code. The Adobe Type Manager parser skips to the first **dup** token after /**Encoding** to find the first character encoding assignment. This sequence of assignments must be followed by an instance of the token **def** or **readonly**; such a token may not occur within the sequence of assignments.

- The only binary data that may occur in a font program are in **Subrs** and **CharStrings** entries.

- The integer immediately following /**Subrs** must be exactly the number of entries in the **Subrs** array.

- Only **Subrs** entries may be defined until the **Subrs** array is completed. Each subroutine is defined using the sequence:

  dup *index nbytes RD ~n~binary~bytes~ NP*

  where *RD* is the name of the procedure performing the **RD** function as defined in section 2.4, "Inside the Encrypted Portion." This is usually either -l or **RD**. *NP* is the name of the procedure performing the **NP** function as defined in section 2.4. This is usually either l or **NP**. There must be exactly one blank between the *RD* token and the binary bytes.

- The integer immediately following /**CharStrings** must be greater than or equal to the number of **CharStrings** entries. Each charstring entry is defined using the sequence:

  charactername nbytes RD ~n~binary~bytes~ ND

  where *charactername* is the name of the character defined by the charstring. *RD* is again the name of the procedure performing the **RD** function as defined in section 2.4. *ND* is the name of the procedure performing the **ND** function as defined in section 2.4. This is usually either |- or **ND**. There must be exactly one blank between the *RD* token and the binary bytes. Only **CharStrings** entries may be defined until the **CharStrings** dictionary is completed.

- The sequence of charstring definitions in the **CharStrings** dictionary must be followed by an instance of the token **end**. An **end** token may not occur within the sequence of **CharStrings** dictionary assignments. No assignments may occur in the Type 1 font program after the **CharStrings** dictionary is completed.

- If the token **FontDirectory** occurs in the font program after the first occurrence of the token /**Private**, then the font program must be a synthetic font, as described in section 9.1, "Synthetic Fonts." If the token **hires** occurs in the font program after the first occurrence of the token /**Private**, then the font must be a hybrid font, as described in section 9.2, "Hybrid Fonts."

Private Dictionary Entries

Entry	Page	Description
BlueFuzz	41	Extends the range of alignment zones. Optional.
BlueScale	39	Related to point size at which to deactivate overshoot suppression. Optional.
BlueShift	40	Overshoot enforcement. If Flex feature is used, then the maximum Flex feature height plus 1. Optional, but relevant even if there is no Flex in the font program.
BlueValues	36	Font-wide vertical alignment zones. Required.
ExpansionFactor	45	Provides control over rendering of counters. Optional.
FamilyBlues	38	Family-wide vertical alignment zones. Optional.
FamilyOtherBlues	38	Family-wide bottom alignment zones. Optional.
ForceBold	43	Set to true to force bold appearance at small sizes. Set to false to inhibit this behavior. Optional.
LanguageGroup	44	Identifies language group of font. Optional.
lenIV	45	Number of bytes at beginning of charstring. Optional.

Entry	*Page*	*Description*
MinFeature	45	Obsolete. Set to {16 16}. Required.
ND	16	Procedure that abbreviates **noaccess def**. Required (may be named I-).
NP	16	Procedure that abbreviates **noaccess put**. Required (may be named I).
OtherBlues	38	Additional bottom alignment zones. Optional.
OtherSubrs	67	Flex, hint replacement, and future extensions. Required if Flex or hint replacement are used.
password	45	Compatibility entry. Set to 5839. Required.
RD	16	Procedure that reads a charstring from the input stream. Required (may be named -I).
RndStemUp	44	Compatibility entry. Use only for font programs in language group 1. Optional.
StdHW	42	Dominant horizontal stem width. Optional.
StdVW	42	Dominant vertical stem width. Optional.
StemSnapH	42	Array of common horizontal stem widths. Optional.
StemSnapV	43	Array of common vertical stem widths. Optional.
Subrs	67	Charstring subroutines. Optional. Required if **OtherSubrs** are used.
UniqueID	17	Number unique to each Type 1 font program. Optional, but strongly recommended.

Charstring Command Values

Value	Command	Value	Command
1	hstem	12 0	dotsection
3	vstem	12 1	vstem3
4	vmoveto	12 2	hstem3
5	rlineto	12 6	seac
6	hlineto	12 7	sbw
7	vlineto	12 12	div
8	rrcurveto	12 16	callothersubr
9	closepath	12 17	pop
10	callsubr	12 33	setcurrentpoint
11	return		
12	escape		
13	hsbw		
14	endchar		
21	rmoveto		
22	hmoveto		
30	vhcurveto		
31	hvcurveto		

APPENDIX 3

OtherSubrs Programs

The following PostScript language code creates four procedures that make up the first four entries in the **OtherSubrs** array in the **Private** dictionary. The first three procedures pertain to Flex and the fourth is used for hint replacement. The code is copyrighted by Adobe Systems Incorporated, and may not be reproduced except by permission of Adobe Systems Incorporated. Adobe Systems Incorporated grants permission to use this code in Type 1 font programs, as long as the code is used as it appears in this document, the copyright notice remains intact, and the character outline code included in such a font program is neither copied nor derived from character outline code in any Adobe Systems font program.

The PostScript language program defining the Flex procedure has been modified since Version 1.0 (March 1990) of this document. Include this code in a font program if you want to use both the Flex and hint replacement features. Another code segment for fonts that require hint replacement only is broken out at the end of this appendix.

The two programs that follow are available on diskette for the convenience of Type 1 font program developers. To order the diskette, please use the order form at the back of this document.

The following code should be executed within the **Private** dictionary:

```
% Copyright (c) 1987-1990 Adobe Systems Incorporated.
% All Rights Reserved.
% This code to be used for Flex and hint replacement.
% Version 1.1
/OtherSubrs
[systemdict /internaldict known
{1183615869 systemdict /internaldict get exec
/FlxProc known {save true} {false} ifelse}
```

```
{userdict /internaldict known not {
userdict /internaldict
{count 0 eq
{/internaldict errordict /invalidaccess get exec} if
dup type /integertype ne
{/internaldict errordict /invalidaccess get exec} if
dup 1183615869 eq
{pop 0}
{/internaldict errordict /invalidaccess get exec}
ifelse
}
dup 14 get 1 25 dict put
bind executeonly put
} if
1183615869 userdict /internaldict get exec
/FlxProc known {save true} {false} ifelse}
ifelse
[
systemdict /internaldict known not
{ 100 dict /begin cvx /mtx matrix /def cvx } if
systemdict /currentpacking known {currentpacking true setpacking} if
{
systemdict /internaldict known {
1183615869 systemdict /internaldict get exec
dup /$FlxDict known not {
dup dup length exch maxlength eq
{ pop userdict dup /$FlxDict known not
{ 100 dict begin /mtx matrix def
dup /$FlxDict currentdict put end } if }
{ 100 dict begin /mtx matrix def
dup /$FlxDict currentdict put end }
ifelse
} if
/$FlxDict get begin
} if
grestore
/exdef {exch def} def
/dmin exch abs 100 div def
/epX exdef /epY exdef
/c4y2 exdef /c4x2 exdef /c4y1 exdef /c4x1 exdef /c4y0 exdef /c4x0 exdef
/c3y2 exdef /c3x2 exdef /c3y1 exdef /c3x1 exdef /c3y0 exdef /c3x0 exdef
/c1y2 exdef /c1x2 exdef /c2x2 c4x2 def /c2y2 c4y2 def
/yflag c1y2 c3y2 sub abs c1x2 c3x2 sub abs gt def
/PickCoords {
{c1x0 c1y0 c1x1 c1y1 c1x2 c1y2 c2x0 c2y0 c2x1 c2y1 c2x2 c2y2 }
{c3x0 c3y0 c3x1 c3y1 c3x2 c3y2 c4x0 c4y0 c4x1 c4y1 c4x2 c4y2 }
ifelse
/y5 exdef /x5 exdef /y4 exdef /x4 exdef /y3 exdef /x3 exdef
/y2 exdef /x2 exdef /y1 exdef /x1 exdef /y0 exdef /x0 exdef
} def
```

```
mtx currentmatrix pop
mtx 0 get abs .00001 lt mtx 3 get abs .00001 lt or
{/flipXY -1 def }
{mtx 1 get abs .00001 lt mtx 2 get abs .00001 lt or
{/flipXY 1 def }
{/flipXY 0 def }
ifelse }
ifelse
/erosion 1 def
systemdict /internaldict known {
1183615869 systemdict /internaldict get exec dup
/erosion known
{/erosion get /erosion exch def}
{pop}
ifelse
} if
yflag
{flipXY 0 eq c3y2 c4y2 eq or
{false PickCoords }
{/shrink c3y2 c4y2 eq
{0}{c1y2 c4y2 sub c3y2 c4y2 sub div abs} ifelse def
/yshrink {c4y2 sub shrink mul c4y2 add} def
/c1y0 c3y0 yshrink def /c1y1 c3y1 yshrink def
/c2y0 c4y0 yshrink def /c2y1 c4y1 yshrink def
/c1x0 c3x0 def /c1x1 c3x1 def /c2x0 c4x0 def /c2x1 c4x1 def
/dY 0 c3y2 c1y2 sub round
dtransform flipXY 1 eq {exch} if pop abs def
dY dmin lt PickCoords
y2 c1y2 sub abs 0.001 gt {
c1x2 c1y2 transform flipXY 1 eq {exch} if
/cx exch def /cy exch def
/dY 0 y2 c1y2 sub round dtransform flipXY 1 eq {exch}
if pop def
dY round dup 0 ne
{/dY exdef }
{pop dY 0 lt {-1}{1} ifelse /dY exdef }
ifelse
/erode PaintType 2 ne erosion 0.5 ge and def
erode {/cy cy 0.5 sub def} if
/ey cy dY add def
/ey ey ceiling ey sub ey floor add def
erode {/ey ey 0.5 add def} if
ey cx flipXY 1 eq {exch} if itransform exch pop
y2 sub /eShift exch def
/y1 y1 eShift add def /y2 y2 eShift add def /y3 y3
eShift add def
} if
} ifelse
}
{flipXY 0 eq c3x2 c4x2 eq or
```

```
{false PickCoords }
{/shrink c3x2 c4x2 eq
{0}{c1x2 c4x2 sub c3x2 c4x2 sub div abs} ifelse def
/xshrink {c4x2 sub shrink mul c4x2 add} def
/c1x0 c3x0 xshrink def /c1x1 c3x1 xshrink def
/c2x0 c4x0 xshrink def /c2x1 c4x1 xshrink def
/c1y0 c3y0 def /c1y1 c3y1 def /c2y0 c4y0 def /c2y1 c4y1 def
/dX c3x2 c1x2 sub round 0 dtransform
flipXY -1 eq {exch} if pop abs def
dX dmin lt PickCoords
x2 c1x2 sub abs 0.001 gt {
c1x2 c1y2 transform flipXY -1 eq {exch} if
/cy exch def /cx exch def
/dX x2 c1x2 sub round 0 dtransform flipXY -1 eq {exch} if pop def
dX round dup 0 ne
{/dX exdef }
{pop dX 0 lt {-1}{1} ifelse /dX exdef }
ifelse
/erode PaintType 2 ne erosion .5 ge and def
erode {/cx cx .5 sub def} if
/ex cx dX add def
/ex ex ceiling ex sub ex floor add def
erode {/ex ex .5 add def} if
ex cy flipXY -1 eq {exch} if itransform pop
x2 sub /eShift exch def
/x1 x1 eShift add def /x2 x2 eShift add def /x3 x3 eShift add def
} if
} ifelse
} ifelse
x2 x5 eq y2 y5 eq or
{ x5 y5 lineto }
{ x0 y0 x1 y1 x2 y2 curveto
x3 y3 x4 y4 x5 y5 curveto }
ifelse
epY epX
}
systemdict /currentpacking known {exch setpacking} if
/exec cvx /end cvx ] cvx
executeonly
exch
{pop true exch restore}
{
systemdict /internaldict known not
{1183615869 userdict /internaldict get exec
exch /FlxProc exch put true}
{1183615869 systemdict /internaldict get exec
dup length exch maxlength eq
{false}
{1183615869 systemdict /internaldict get exec
exch /FlxProc exch put true}
```

```
ifelse}
ifelse}
ifelse
{systemdict /internaldict known
{{1183615869 systemdict /internaldict get exec /FlxProc get exec}}
{{1183615869 userdict /internaldict get exec /FlxProc get exec}}
ifelse executeonly
} if
{gsave currentpoint newpath moveto} executeonly
{currentpoint grestore gsave currentpoint newpath moveto} executeonly
{systemdict /internaldict known not
{pop 3}
{1183615869 systemdict /internaldict get exec
dup /startlock known
{/startlock get exec}
{dup /strtlck known
{/strtlck get exec}
{pop 3}
ifelse}
ifelse}
ifelse
} executeonly
] noaccess def
```

For hint replacement only, use this code:

```
% Copyright (c) 1987 Adobe Systems Incorporated.
% All rights reserved.
% This code to be used for hint replacement only.
/OtherSubrs
[{} {} {}
{systemdict /internaldict known not
{pop 3}
{1183615869 systemdict /internaldict get exec
dup /startlock known
{/startlock get exec}
{dup /strtlck known
{/strtlck get exec}
{pop 3}
ifelse}
ifelse}
ifelse
} executeonly
] noaccess def
```

The first listing of PostScript language code creates an array of four elements, each of which is a procedure, and it associates this array with **OtherSubrs**. Some of this code is executed when the font program is read. At that time, a somewhat complicated selection of the correct procedure to place in slot 0 is made. This selection is based on features that may or may not be present in various versions of the PostScript interpreter.

If the Flex mechanism is not used in the font program, entries 0, 1, and 2 may be replaced by null procedures ({ }). If hint replacement is not used in the font program, entry 3 may be eliminated. If neither Flex nor hint replacement is used, the **OtherSubrs** array may be eliminated entirely.

The preceding code uses a special dictionary, **internaldict** for several operators and values. This dictionary has limited capacity and the PostScript interpreter depends on its integrity for correct operation. Do not use this dictionary for any purpose other than as part of the preceding code. Furthermore, if you write your own code for these functions, do not use the name **FlxProc**; this may interfere with other font programs that incorporate the preceding code.

Changes

This document describes Version 1.1 of the *Adobe Type 1 Font Format*. Changes to the *Adobe Type 1 Font Format* from Version 1.0 published March 1990, are noted in the paragraphs below.

Clearly documented default values for the **BlueScale** (.039625), **BlueShift** (7), **BlueFuzz** (1), and **ExpansionFactor** (.06) entries in the Private dictionary. See pages 40-41, and 45.

A new entry to the **Private** dictionary, **ExpansionFactor**, provides a font level hint that is useful for intelligent rendering of character glyphs such as bar codes and logos that have a lot of counters. See page 45.

Added warning to the description of the **closepath** command about using closepath to form a subpath section intended to be zero length. See page 51.

The Adobe Type Manager parser skips to the first **dup** token after **/Encoding** to find the first character encoding assignment. See page 85.

The PostScript language program defining the Flex procedure in Appendix 3 has been modified to protect against trying to put the **$FlxDict** into **internaldict** if **internaldict** is full. The old code could lead to **dictfull** errors out of **show** in certain unlikely circumstances. The new code simply puts the **$FlxDict** in **userdict** if **internaldict** is full. See pages 91-95.

Index

Colophon

This book was produced using FrameMaker 2.0 and other application software packages that support the PostScript language and Type 1 font programs. Camera-ready film masters were produced on a high-resolution PostScript imagesetter.

The type used is entirely from the *ITC Stone®* family, designed at Adobe Systems. Chapter headings are set in *ITC Stone Sans Semibold* 24 point and the body text is set in 10 on 12 point *ITC Stone Serif*, *ITC Stone Serif Italic* and *ITC Stone Sans Semibold*.

Authors—Doug Brotz, Bill Paxton, Jeff Walden

Editing—Jeff Walden, Judith Walthers von Alten

Index—Minette Norman, Sue Crisman, Laura Dower

Illustrations—Keala Hagman, Kim Isola, Rob Babcock

Cover Design—Nancy Winters, Donna Helliwell

Book Design—Nancy Winters, Eve Lynes

Book Production—Andrea Bruno, Eve Lynes, Robin Edwards, Laura Dower, Lisa Kelly.

Technical Assistance—Dick Sweet, Andy Shore

Reviewers—Rob Babcock, Doug Brotz, Bill Paxton, Kathe Morris, Terry O'Donnell, Linda Weinert, Linda Gass, Mike Byron, Peter Hibbard, Dan Mills, David Lemon, Ed Taft, Matt Foley

Publication Management—Eve Lynes, Joan Delfino

Product Management—Rob Babcock

Diskette Order Form

If you send this coupon (or a copy of it) to Adobe Systems, we will send you a diskette containing the PostScript language programs listed in Appendix 3 that pertain to Flex and hint replacement.

TYPE 1 DISKETTE OFFER - VERSION 1.1

Please send me a copy of the program diskette. I have enclosed $10.00 to cover the costs of materials, handling, and postage. Thank you.

❑ 3-1/2" Macintosh format ❑ 5-1/4" PC format

Name _____

Title _____

Organization _____

Street _____

City _____ *State* _____ *Zip* _____

Phone _____

Mail to: Type 1 Diskette Offer
Adobe Systems Incorporated
P.O. Box 7900
Mountain View, CA 94039-7900